Angela Elvira

Con mucho aprecio

John

Ann

About the authors

John Crabtree is a research associate at the Latin American Centre, Oxford, and a senior member of St Antony's College. His main area of expertise is the contemporary politics of the Andean region, on which he has written and broadcast widely. His most recent books include *Fractured Politics: Peruvian Democracy Past and Present* (2011) and *Unresolved Tensions: Bolivia Past and Present* (2008), co-edited with Laurence Whitehead. In 2005 he published *Patterns of Protest: Politics and Social Movements in Bolivia*. He holds a master's degree from Liverpool University and a doctorate from Oxford Brookes University.

Ann Chaplin has lived and worked in Bolivia and the Andes for many years. She has worked in development, relating closely to social movements, and has been a witness to their advances. She has written recently on the development of social movements and the impact of climate change on rural communities.

GW00471278

BOLIVIA PROCESSES OF CHANGE

John Crabtree and Ann Chaplin

Zed Books

LONDON | NEW YORK

Bolivia: Processes of change was first published in 2013 by Zed Books Ltd, 7 Cynthia Street, London N1 9JF, UK and Room 400, 175 Fifth Avenue, New York, NY 10010, USA

www.zedbooks.co.uk

FSC
www.fsc.org
MIX
Paper from
responsible sources
FSC® C013604

Set in Monotype Plantin and FFKievit by Ewan Smith, London NW5
Index: ed.emery@thefreeuniversity.net
Cover design: www.roguefour.co.uk
Printed and bound in Great Britain by CPI Group (UK) Ltd, Croydon, CRO 4YY

Distributed in the USA exclusively by Palgrave Macmillan, a division of St Martin's Press, LLC, 175 Fifth Avenue, New York, NY 10010, USA

A catalogue record for this book is available from the British Library
Library of Congress Cataloging in Publication Data available

ISBN 978 1 78032 377 0 hb
ISBN 978 1 78032 376 3 pb

CONTENTS

PROLOGUE

Of all the countries of Latin America, in recent years Bolivia has been among those that have gone farthest in the search for new policies to confront old problems. The government of Evo Morales Ayma – first elected in 2005 with 54 per cent of the popular vote and then re-elected in 2009 with 64 per cent – has sought to abandon the narrowly orthodox economic path previously advocated by the IMF and the World Bank. It has challenged the right of the United States to dictate drug eradication policies with respect to the cultivation of coca, the raw material for cocaine. It has taken steps to industrialize some of its commodity exports, and thereby boost retained earnings. It has adopted a strident tone in the international debates surrounding climate change. It has sought to broaden its international relations, seeking to develop ties with countries with which, previously, there was little contact. But perhaps most significantly, Bolivia has captured the attention of the world owing to the new areas of political and social participation it has spearheaded in its domestic policies, particularly among indigenous groups, which, although forming the majority of the population, have traditionally been marginalized from decision-making by the country's political elites. Evo Morales, whose own background was one of dire poverty and whose emergence as a political leader owed nothing to connivance with traditional elites, represents a new sort of leadership in Latin American politics. His electoral successes provided eloquent testimony of a legitimacy that had been patently lacking among his predecessors as president during the previous twenty years.

At the same time, the experience of the Morales administration since 2006 has drawn attention to the difficulties involved in bringing change in the patterns of development in one of Latin America's poorest and most unequal countries. The purpose of this book is to examine these difficulties, and the advances made, through the experiences of ordinary people in different parts of the country. Bolivia is a country in which popular organization is strong, and where social movements of one kind or another have long had a major impact on politics and decision-making. The book therefore examines the evolution of these movements and how the lives of those people involved have been affected – for better or for worse – by their participation. It is a story, therefore, of empowerment and social advance, not least in material well-being. But it is also a story of inevitable frustrations and the inability to achieve all the advances that people naturally aspire to, particularly given the huge expectations generated by the election of Morales as president.

The book is not a chronicle of the Morales administration as such, though the experiences of ordinary people clearly throw light on the many significant developments that have taken place in the country since 2006. Nor is it the personal story of Evo Morales himself. Other writers have written on these themes. What we seek to do in this book is, through interviews with those involved with and in social movements, to gauge the extent to which people's lives have been affected – whether positively or negatively – by the changes that have taken place, and how they perceive those changes. By so doing, it seeks to shine light on the relationships between people, social movements and the state, highlighting in the process the achievements and the limitations of the MAS government.

The book is structured around the experiences of individuals and social movements in different parts of the country, reflecting the heterogeneity of organizations and their views about their own reality. The chapters therefore follow a geographical logic, using regions to highlight specific and more general problems. Our visits to these different parts of Bolivia hammered home to us the need to distinguish clearly between one region and another, and to avoid the overly generalized approach that characterizes a good deal of writing about Bolivian politics. At the same time, however, we have sought to use these regional profiles to highlight more general themes that are relevant to the country's political evolution and its socio-economic development. We are interested in how people's living conditions have changed in recent years, how their quality of life has changed, what concepts like *vivir bien* mean to them, the extent to which they feel empowered by the acquisition of new rights, and what participation in social movements at different moments and in different contexts has meant to them in practice. We are also interested in general issues, such as how the country's development trajectory benefits people, or not, and the policy dilemmas and disagreements that have arisen. Many of these problems are ones that also affect other countries in Latin America, and Bolivia's experience has considerable relevance for the rest of Latin America, and even for developing countries farther afield. No country is an island, particularly one which, as in this case, is landlocked.

The book opens, however, with two chapters of a more general nature, which we feel is essential to an understanding of contemporary politics in different parts of the country. Unlike the chapters that follow, they are based less on interview material. The first of these relates to the history of popular organization and collective action which has typified Bolivia, and which – to some extent – differentiates it from its South American neighbours. This legacy of social organization, and the conquests to which it has given rise, is key to an understanding of current politics; together they inform the country's political culture. Though the Morales administration may seek to underscore its 'revolutionary' credentials, it is our belief that it forms a part of an ongoing historical continuum of which it is but the latest chapter. The second involves a more specific analysis of problems of indigenous rights and landholding in Bolivia, problems which also have been long in gestation. In order to make sense of some of the conflicts that have emerged in recent times at the local level – particularly between campesinos and indigenous peoples – it is important to understand how changes in patterns of landholding have affected different groups in different places. This is not just a 'rural' problem, but one that crucially affects patterns of migration and urbanization.

The number and variety of people we talked to – 160 in all – hopefully highlight the fact that different people in different places face different problems and use different approaches to resolve these problems. We have obviously been selective about the issues we chose to raise and the places we decided to visit. Through our travels to different places, we feel we have covered a significant range of situations, striking a balance between rural and urban, highland and lowland. The places we visited and the people we met were an inspiration to us both, helping us to deepen our knowledge of the country and those who live in it.

The interviews on which this book are based were carried out in the first half of 2012, a period when the government faced a testing time in providing responses to the various challenges facing it from social movements and other sectors of the population. The sense of heady optimism that had characterized the first period in government gave way to a climate of questioning and growing criticism of the government and its policies. This comes across in many of the interviews, with many sectors showing themselves frustrated that the promises of the new era were proving far harder to fulfil than expected. Though the economy continued to grow, the material benefits for ordinary Bolivians were not as high as many had hoped. There remained real limits to the extent of participation in decision-making. And for many on the left, the government failed to achieve that break with neoliberalism and global capitalism which its rhetoric had proposed. In short, the 'process of change' proved more difficult to achieve in practice than its more optimistic advocates had originally envisaged.

Still, as the interviews also show, there were important changes during these years that will probably prove difficult to reverse. In this sense we talk about 'processes of change' rather than the 'process of change'. Social and cultural barriers that had excluded sectors from decision-making were lifted. New actors had emerged on the scene, empowered by government policies; others, important in the past, were sidelined. Poverty rates were reduced, as were some of the regional inequalities that had for so long plagued Bolivia's pattern of development. That the process of change was less than revolutionary and that there were important continuities with the past perhaps goes without saying; but for many – perhaps most – Bolivians, this was a period when ordinary people felt the benefits of policy in ways that had not been the case for decades, if ever. It provided a particularly telling moment, therefore, to probe beneath the surface of political opinion and to ask people what they thought of the changes of the previous six years, how these had affected their lives and the extent to which they felt they had a voice in the 'new' Bolivia. As might be expected in such a heterogeneous country, the responses were far from uniform.

As well as acknowledging all those who gave us their time and judgements (the complete list of those we interviewed is included at the end of this book), we would like to identify those whose views helped us orient this study and to provide us with the contacts at the local level which made it possible. They include Xavier Albó, Helena Argirakis, Judith Cóndor Vidal, Denise Humphries Bebbington, Roxana Liendo, Marcos Nordgren, José Pimentel, Carlos Revilla and Alison Spedding, who gave us their comments and useful insights on specific chapters. Susana Eróstegui and Fany Cárdenas were most generous with contacts, as were José Luis Alvarez, Juan José Avila, Denise Bebbington, Alfredo Cahuaya, Eva Colque, Rodolfo Eróstegui, Javier Gómez, Marcos Nordgren and Godofredo Sandóval. It must be said that the views (and final interpretations) expressed here are our own, not necessarily those of the people who contributed to this book. We would also like to acknowledge the financial help we received from Oxfam GB, which helped us cover the costs of travel to different parts of the country. Without such assistance the book would have been much more difficult to write.

La Paz, November 2012

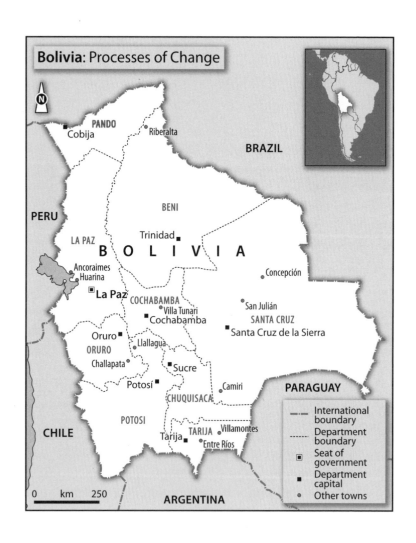

Bolivia: Processes of Change

N

PERU

PANDO
Cobija ■
Riberalta ●

BRAZIL

BENI

LA PAZ
Trinidad ■

B O L I V I A

Ancoraimes ●
Huarina ●
◘ **La Paz**

Concepción ●

COCHABAMBA
Villa Tunari ●
Cochabamba ■

San Julián ●
SANTA CRUZ
Santa Cruz de la Sierra ■

Oruro ■
ORURO
Challapata ●
Llallagua ●

Sucre ■

Potosí ■
Camiri ●

CHUQUISACA

PARAGUAY

POTOSI

CHILE

Tarija ■
TARIJA
Villamontes ●
Entre Ríos ●

	International boundary
	Department boundary
◘	Seat of government
■	Department capital
●	Other towns

0   km   250

ARGENTINA

INTRODUCTION: POPULAR ORGANIZATION AND THE PROCESSES OF CHANGE

To understand the changes which Bolivia has been experiencing in recent years, we believe that it is first necessary to underscore the role played by popular mobilization and collective action in the history of the country, particularly over the last half-century. In this Introduction, therefore, we seek to sketch in some of the defining characteristics of social movements as they evolved over the twentieth and early twenty-first centuries. Bolivia, indeed, stands out in Latin America, for the strength and assertiveness of its social movements in achieving major social conquests, and the experiences of the past colour those of the present. As we shall see, social movements of different sorts have had a direct and powerful influence over the country's politics. Though political culture is something that is difficult to define in very precise terms, the legacies from the past crucially affect how people see the present and how they visualize their own role within the political process. The ability of social organization to survive repeated attempts to suppress it at different points over the last few decades underscores both its strong roots in civil society and the relative weakness of the state in imposing its agenda on an organized workforce which has managed to retain much of its autonomy of action.

The National Revolution of April 1952 stands like a watershed in the history of Bolivia in the twentieth century. It was then that mineworkers, other sectors of the workforce and disgruntled sectors of the middle class took up arms against the elite-based system of governance that preceded the revolution. Armed mainly with Mausers dating from the 1930s, militias succeeded in subduing Bolivia's rag-bag armed forces, deposing the government which had imposed itself by electoral fraud a year earlier. The Movimiento Nacionalista Revolucionario (MNR), a party born in the 1940s, took power, with Víctor Paz Estenssoro, a middle-class lawyer, becoming president.

It expressed a strongly nationalistic ideology, based on an alliance of different social classes: workers, peasants and the middle class. Paz was to remain a central figure in Bolivian politics almost until his death at the age of ninety-three in 2001, having been president for four separate periods. But the 1952 revolution, one of the few genuine social revolutions in twentieth-century Latin America, did not take place out of the blue. It was a consequence of the process of social change that had been taking place in the country over several decades, particularly since the disastrous Chaco War against Paraguay (1932–35), which acted as a catalyst for social mobilization and demonstrated with brutal clarity the ineffectiveness and corruption of the *ancien régime*. Bolivia, more than perhaps any other Latin American country, showed the strength of popular organization, built around the mineworkers, and the weakness of state structures in a country whose main source of wealth was the personal property of three men and their business empires, the so-called Tin Barons.

In particular, the period after the Chaco War saw the development of social organization in the main mining encampments, many of them far from the centres of political control. Mineworkers, by the nature of their occupation and the strong presence of political parties in their midst, exhibited levels of social solidarity and political acumen that were atypical of the population as a whole. Strikes and struggles for basic labour rights were commonplace in the country's main mining centres. A milestone in the development of trade unionism in Bolivia was the foundation in 1944 of the mineworkers' federation, the Federación Sindical de Trabajadores Mineros de Bolivia (FSTMB). This followed nearly three years after the government of the time sent in troops to quell a strike in the country's largest mining complex, owned by Patiño Mines, the so-called Massacre of Catavi (1942). The Bolivian mineworkers became one of the most politicized sectors of the workforce anywhere in Latin America. The Thesis of Pulacayo, adopted by the FSTMB at its Congress in 1946, was a particularly radical document; it revealed the strength of Trotskyist influence among organized labour, a phenomenon without parallel elsewhere in the region. As 1952 was to show, the Bolivian mineworkers could take on the state and win.

But the miners were not the only organized sector of the workforce in 1952. During the previous period, peasants too had been able to organize and make important advances. This was particularly the case in the valley of Cochabamba, Bolivia's breadbasket at the time, where peasants had successfully come together to take control of the landed estates on which they worked in conditions of virtual serfdom. The extent of rural militancy was less notable at the time in the highland Altiplano, but there was a strong legacy of social organization dating from pre-Columbian times and resistance (sometimes violent) to the social inroads of private property into a structure of communitarian agriculture based on the traditional *ayllu*. Though peasants did not play a major role in the events of 1952, they were the beneficiaries of an agrarian reform, decreed in 1953, which brought to an end the pattern of agricultural domination based around the hacienda, replacing it with small-scale family-based property ownership. Indeed, the MNR in its approach sought to highlight the role of the 'campesino' and to downplay that of indigenous identity in rural politics.

Following the nationalization of the property of the Tin Barons in 1952 and the establishment of the Corporación Minera de Bolivia (Comibol), the mineworkers and their union, the FSTMB, became powerful actors within the politics of the country. As the MNR, aided and abetted by the United States, moved to the right, sharp frictions arose between the miners and the government. The notion of 'co-government', a key point of the Thesis of Pulacayo, was quickly dropped, but the newly formed Central Obrera Boliviana (COB) was assertive in protecting workers' rights. Unlike in other countries in Latin America, the COB managed to maintain its institutional unity and to resist attempts by parties on the left to carve up the union movement between them. However, the notion of a worker–peasant alliance was always shaky, particularly given the attempts by the MNR (and subsequently by military governments) to co-opt the peasant union movement that emerged strengthened by the agrarian reform. The high point of the COB's influence came with the Asamblea Popular in 1970/71, when the notion of co-government re-emerged with force during the short-lived left-wing military government of General Juan José Torres. During the right-wing military regimes of General René Barrientos (1964–69) and General Hugo Banzer (1971–78), the labour movement as a whole faced harassment by the state – and some notable massacres in the mines, such as the Massacre of San Juan (in June 1967), and the imprisonment and exile of many of the key miners' leaders. Still, the relative weakness of the state, as opposed to the unions and other social movements, was made manifest in 1978 when, following lengthy hunger strikes and other forms of protest, the Banzer regime found itself obliged to call elections and the military, following the collapse of the García Meza dictatorship, eventually withdrew to their barracks in 1982.

It was in the early 1980s that the strength of the union movement was tested – this time not by the military – and was found wanting. The experience of hyperinflation in 1983–85 during the left-wing government of the Unidad Democrática y Popular (UDP) undermined the capacity of the union movement to negotiate wages and labour conditions. While the COB found it difficult to keep abreast of the reduction in the value of real wages, it also undermined the government which it started out supporting. In 1984, President Hernán Siles Zuazo, a veteran of 1952, was forced to call early elections, elections won by his erstwhile partner in 1952, Víctor Paz Estenssoro. The Paz administration ushered in a wholesale liberalization of the economy, in which the FSTMB, the COB and other labour organizations were the main victims. Enthusiastically supported by the IMF and the World Bank, Paz presided over the liberalization of the labour market and the suppression of acquired worker rights. Faced with a savage decline in the world tin price, the Paz government oversaw the closure of almost all the state-owned mining sector, expelling some 27,000 mineworkers from their jobs and reducing Comibol to the shell of an organization. When prices subsequently picked up, it was the private sector which was the main beneficiary. While the COB routinely staged acts of protest against the government's economic policies, without the mineworkers it lacked the force to exert significant influence on policy.

The period of neoliberalism probably reached its peak during the first government of Gonzalo Sánchez de Lozada (1993–97). Sánchez de Lozada, or 'Goni' as he is often called, one of Bolivia's wealthiest mining entrepreneurs and the architect of the reforms of the 1985–89 Paz Estenssoro government, pushed ahead with the privatization of Bolivia's main state companies, most importantly the state oil and gas company, Yacimientos Petrolíferos Fiscales Bolivianos (YPFB), measures opposed by the COB but without much impact. Sánchez de Lozada sought to make the reforms irreversible, partly by promising to use the resources generated by privatization to establish social welfare funds through what he called 'capitalization'. He also pushed ahead with 'second generation reforms' aimed at building a new liberal institutionality, particularly with respect to local government, through his Participación Popular scheme and through administrative and fiscal decentralization. But neoliberalism never lived up to the exaggerated promises made when it was enacted. Employment, contrary to promises, failed to increase. Wages stagnated in real terms, and many of the social gains made in previous decades were reversed. The liberalization of the labour market meant, in effect, increased job insecurity in a country where much of the labour market was already in the so-called informal sector. Indices of poverty and inequality increased during these years.

But the apparent quiescence of popular organizations in these years proved illusory. Beneath the surface, changes were afoot, changes that were dramatically to modify the political scene in the early years of the new millennium. First, the peasant movement, which had been largely co-opted in the years after 1952, began to show new signs of independence. The growth of *indigenismo* in the rural sector dated back to the 1970s, when the Katarista movement began to organize the peasantry of the Altiplano along lines of Aymara ethnicity. In 1979, a new peasant federation, the Confederación Sindical Unica de Trabajadores Campesinos de Bolivia (CSUTCB), came into being, with a blend of ethnic and class-based ideologies. In the tropics of La Paz, Cochabamba and Santa Cruz, a union federation of migrants from the highlands, the Confederación Sindical de Colonizadores de Bolivia (CSCB), also became an influential actor, and the coca producers (*cocaleros*) were part of this organization. Both movements were represented within the COB. Secondly, the closure of most of the public sector mines in and after 1985 led to the dispersal of this politicized and highly organized workforce to other parts of the country, taking their union traditions with them. Some migrated to the Chapare district of Cochabamba, where coca cultivation was rapidly in the ascendant at the time. Others found refuge in the urban townships surrounding the country's main cities, especially in El Alto, the sprawling suburb that spreads out across the Altiplano from La Paz, the seat of government. Thirdly, Participación Popular and the decentralization that went with it led to the growth of more assertiveness at the local level. Municipalities were given more resources than before and grassroots organizations were granted the facility to oversee the activities of local municipalities. And fourthly, by 1990 there were signs of consolidation of a movement of indigenous peoples of the lowlands in the eastern half of the country, whose voice had previously gone unheard. A landmark march of indigenous peoples from Trinidad, the capital city of the Beni, to La Paz – just over six hundred kilometres away – showed that some new actors had also come of age. Finally, regional movements, such as those which organized around the privatization of water in Cochabamba, and also in El Alto against the introduction of new municipal taxes, began to make their voices heard.

It was in these circumstances that the MAS (the Movimiento al Socialismo – Instrumento Político para la Soberanía de los Pueblos, MAS-IPSP – to give it its full name) came into being. The IPSP sobriquet is significant. Those involved in this movement did not wish to call themselves a political party as such. Political parties at this time had gained an unwholesome reputation for using public office for the personal benefit of their leaders and for their failure to represent social interests. Originally dating from 1995 and called the Asamblea por la Soberanía de los Pueblos, the political grouping that was to become the MAS drew on the union structure that prevailed among the coca farmers of the Chapare. By 1995, several years had passed since the closure of the state mining sector, and the form of organization adopted by the coca farmers of the Chapare bore all the familiar hallmarks of mining trade unionism. The MAS was originally conceived of as the 'political instrument' of peasants and coca producers, reflecting the long-held view that syndicalism was not just a defensive mechanism to protect the interests of a specific sector of workers, but the means through which to fight for permanent change in the political domain. It is worth mentioning that, with the exception of brief experiences of guerrilla warfare – starting with Che Guevara's ill-fated venture in

Bolivia of the 1960s – the union movement was largely resistant to insurrectional politics.

The MAS proved a dynamic new force in Bolivian politics. It was established as such at the time of the 1997 elections, in which it won the enthusiastic backing of those living in the Cochabamba tropics but relatively little elsewhere. By the time of the 1999 municipal elections, it had spread its influence beyond the Chapare, but failed to win strong support in the country's main urban capitals. With the 2002 presidential elections, however, it came within an ace of winning the presidency, with Evo Morales as its presidential candidate. In the end, Sánchez de Lozada pipped Morales to the post by only a narrow margin (22.9 to 20.9 per cent). Overnight, the MAS became the country's second-largest party, eclipsing well-established parties such as the MNR, the Movimiento de Izquierda Revolucionaria (MIR) of former president Jaime Paz Zamora, and Acción Democrática Nacionalista (ADN) of former president Hugo Banzer, who had succeeded Sánchez de Lozada in 1997.

The success of the MAS was, in part, a function of the crisis of the political parties that had dominated the system since the return to democracy in the 1980s and had shared political power between them and the spoils that went with it; but it was also the ability to take advantage of the wave of protests that emerged in Bolivia after 1999, to provide a political platform for them and to create a national political force with an appeal in most, if not all, parts of the country. The MAS was able to 'join up the dots' of individual protest movements and to produce an ideology with a broad political appeal, combining a well-honed resort to nationalism with a new blend of indigenous politics. The campaign against coca eradication in the Chapare that first brought it to national prominence included both elements: a strident anti-US appeal combined with a reverence for the coca leaf as a symbol of Bolivia's indigenous identity and that of the majority of its people.

The process by which different protest movements built on one another between 1999 and 2003 has been dealt with in an earlier book (*Patterns of Protest: Politics and Social Movements in Bolivia*, Latin America Bureau, 2004). Suffice it to say here that the victory of a variety of social and popular movements in Cochabamba in 1999 and 2000

– the so-called Water War – in opposition to the privatization of the local water and sanitation system exposed the weakness of the government of the time. At much the same time, peasants spearheaded a series of protests against low agricultural prices and other demands, while the coca producers rallied against the eradication of their crop and in favour of legalizing small areas of coca production (the *cato*).

The activities of these protest movements reached a climax in October 2003, when, following government plans to sell Bolivian gas supplies to the United States via Chile, there was a social explosion in El Alto which led, after the killing of sixty-seven protesters, to the ousting of Sánchez de Lozada and his government. It gave rise to a series of demands that became known as the 'October Agenda', a set of proposals that was to guide the MAS administration after it won power in the landslide elections of 2005. The protest movements had a dynamic of their own, even though MAS supporters were involved in many of them. Indeed, in the 2003 Gas War which toppled the government, Evo Morales was conspicuous by his absence. However, in electoral terms, Morales was able to capitalize on the mood of discontent and articulate a discourse that chimed with the quest for alternatives to what had gone before. Other leaders of protest movements failed to project an appeal that went beyond that of a narrow-interest group. The example of Felipe Quispe, the campesino leader of Aymaran 'nationalism' who had been behind several bouts of protest on the Altiplano in the period after the Cochabamba Water War, is a case in point. He failed to create an appeal that went beyond his own rather narrow ethnic constituency. Whereas Morales won nearly 54 per cent of the vote nationwide in the 2005 elections, Quispe managed barely 2 per cent.

By 2003, then, the nature of popular organization and mobilization had changed significantly, in that the base of organization had widened to include sectors of the population that had not previously been key actors. This was particularly the case in the rural sphere, which was to become a core area of electoral support for the MAS. Organizations like the CSUTCB, the Confederación de Colonizadores, the Federación Nacional de Mujeres Campesinas Bartolina Sisa, and – of course – the *cocaleros*, were the organizational building blocks on which the MAS was based. With the exception of El Alto, its urban support was consolidated later between 2003 and the elections of 2005 when a number of middle-class politicians were 'invited' to join the MAS electoral slate. The methods of popular protest had also changed significantly. As well as time-honoured forms such as strikes, hunger strikes and marches, the blocking of roads became one of the hallmarks of protest at this time. The *bloqueo* was an effective method by which peasants could interrupt commercial activity – often for days on end – and thus exercise political leverage. Given the relative paucity of road communications in Bolivia, it was particularly effective. Blocking the main road through the Chapare, for instance, could interrupt most commerce between the lowlands of Santa Cruz and much of the rest of the country.

The October Agenda was to set the framework for politics for the following years. A key demand of the protesters in El Alto was the convening of a Constituent Assembly to revise the existing constitution – which in essence dated from 1967 – and to incorporate within it a new charter of indigenous rights. This was not a new demand – it had been one of the key points of the march from Trinidad in 1990 – but it had gained momentum in the meantime. The 2001 census, for instance, had pointed to the fact that 62 per cent of the population self-identified as indigenous, even though the methodology of the census has been questioned by some. Another demand was the renationalizing of the gas industry, effectively privatized under Sánchez de Lozada as a result of his 'capitalization' scheme. Angered by suggestions of corruption in the deals forged with foreign companies, the protesters demanded that the state should take control of the country's hydrocarbons resources, the main source of export revenue. Thirdly, and related to the previous point, the October Agenda sought to reorient the economy away from the neoliberal model, reviving a tradition of state intervention and giving Bolivian citizens a greater say over how their economy was to be developed. This agenda had immediate effect in forcing Goni's successor, Carlos Mesa, into holding a five-point referendum on the hydrocarbons issue. On the question of the Constituent Assembly, one of Evo Morales's first acts as president was to set in motion the timetable and procedures by which such an assembly would be elected. By 2009 these demands had largely been met, though a further demand, the extradition of Goni for the killings of October 2003, had not been accomplished.

The government of Evo Morales and the MAS was officially inaugurated in January 2006. It represented a turning point in Bolivian politics, both symbolically and in reality. The symbolism of an indigenous peasant becoming president of Bolivia echoed around the world. It finally broke the idea that only those with a white skin and a formal education could take over executive functions. It smashed the 'glass ceiling', probably for ever. At an evocative celebration in the pre-Columbian ruins of Tiwanaku the day before his inauguration, Morales laid claim to his indigenous ancestry before a crowd which included representatives of indigenous peoples from across the Americas (including the United States and Canada). The reality of the change of government was just as dramatic as the symbolism. The new cabinet included many representatives of social movements which had supported the campaign of the MAS. Some of these had little by way of previous experience in government, though several had experience working in NGOs. The composition of the National Congress was a far cry from that of its predecessors, with the MAS achieving a majority in the Chamber of Deputies and only narrowly missing a majority in the Senate. It was no longer a club restricted to political elites, and though the MAS presence in parliament was by no means drawn entirely from people of popular extraction, it was far more representative of ordinary Bolivians than it had ever been before.

The relationship between the MAS and the social movements that had brought it to power is not necessarily clear cut. As the next few years were to show, this relationship came under strain as the government took decisions that angered some sectional interests. Likewise, the government was not always able to meet popular demands that had been built up over decades. There were, from the start, some social movements that kept a certain distance from the government, concerned to maintain a degree of autonomy. This was the case at times, for example, with the Confederación de Pueblos Indígenas de Bolivia (Cidob), a confederation representing the numerous indigenous peoples of lowland Bolivia, mainly from the departments of Beni, Pando, Santa Cruz and Tarija. As we have mentioned, those most closely integrated into the MAS included the *cocaleros*, the CSUTCB peasant confederation, the *colonizadores* (now called Comunidades Interculturales) and the Bartolina Sisa peasant women's federation. The position of the COB, now a much less influential body than in the past, was more ambivalent, depending on its own internal politics and the relationship with the government with respect to issues such as wage policy. While the MAS claimed to be a 'party of the social movements', the relationship between them has been erratic and fluctuating. When it came to defending the interests of a particular social movement, this took precedence over blind support for the government. The relationship was therefore never highly institutionalized. The nearest attempt to developing an instance of coordination between the MAS and the social movements came with the creation of Conalcam (the Coordinadora Nacional por el Cambio) in 2007; this body met more regularly during Morales's first government.

Implementation of the October Agenda – specifically the process of electing a Constituent Assembly and the subsequent rewriting of the constitution on the one hand, and the 'renationalization' of Bolivia's hydrocarbons resources on the other – did much to solidify the relationship between the government and social movements. The slogan 'Bolivia Avanza – Evo Cumple' (Bolivia Advances, Evo Fulfils His Promises) – the name given to a programme of social works projects – had considerable resonance, at least for the duration of Morales's first administration (2006–10). At the same time, support for the government was buttressed by the activities of those on the right, keen to undermine the government and its agenda of change. Opposition to the process of constitutional change being discussed within the Assembly effectively polarized the country, particularly with respect to the pretensions of elites in the so-called '*media luna*' in the eastern lowlands to pursue policies of autonomy that threatened to subvert the objectives of the new constitution. This polarization reached a climax in September 2008 when the opposition set in motion widespread acts of violence in towns and cities of the Oriente in open defiance of the government. Such tactics did much to reinforce the support of social movements and others for the government. At the same time, Morales, evoking nationalist sentiments, was able to point to the activities of the US government, through its embassy in La Paz, in exacerbating such difficulties. As always, the role of outside intervention in Bolivia's internal politics provided a potent rallying cry in a country overly accustomed to outsiders intervening in its domestic affairs.

The extent to which Morales's election and the activities of his government led to greater social inclusion and the further empowerment of social movements is a central theme of this book. Access to decision-making certainly increased, and the government was keen to create new channels of representation that had not existed before. From the start, Morales sought to identify closely with social movements, tirelessly travelling the country and associating himself with these and their leaders. This was a far cry from the traditional activities of presidents who, once elected, tended to turn their backs on those who had voted for them. Access to government also brought with it access to resources which social movements had previously lacked. But at the same time, winning power had negative effects for social organizations. Many of the leaders of social movements found themselves taking up roles in government or the legislature, creating problems in terms of finding people to replace them. Problems also emerged of co-optation and, in some instances, corruption, whereby the temptations of office proved too much for those exposed to them. Dependence on close relations with government could, in some circumstances, end up weakening or dividing social movements. Moving from 'protest mode' to government, from *protesta* to *propuesta*, was not without its problems for popular organizations and their development.

Another major problem, particularly for the government, emerged when conflicts within or between social movements broke out. An example of this, as we shall see in Chapter 5, was the conflict in October 2006 between different sectors of the workforce at the Huanuni mine, the only state-run mining operation to avoid closure in the mid-1980s and one of Bolivia's largest extant tin operations. The recovery of tin prices, alongside other minerals prices, had led to large numbers of '*cooperativistas*' seeking to work the mine's plentiful ores. Because of their number, not just at Huanuni but throughout the mining sector, the *cooperativistas* became an important bastion of support for the government. At Huanuni, though, they clashed with the unionized workforce, one of the few remaining props of the once mighty FSTMB, which had continued to work the mine. In the battle that ensued for control of one of Huanuni's most productive veins, seventeen workers lost their lives and many more were injured. Faced with the dilemma of which sector of the workforce to support, the government finally responded by taking most of the *cooperativistas* on to the government payroll.

The new constitution, ratified by referendum in January 2009, represented an important departure from its predecessors, particularly with respect to enhancing the rights of indigenous peoples. Of course, how these rights would be implemented and interpreted judicially would depend on subsequent legislation, and the passage of such legislation would be a major preoccupation for the legislature, renamed the Plurinational Legislative Assembly, during Morales's second administration beginning in January 2010. The constitutional document is a long one, consisting of 411 articles. The original document approved by a majority of the members of the Constituent Assembly, but not the opposition minority, underwent some important changes in the process of subsequent negotiations, required to win opposition agreement for the final text. From our standpoint here, perhaps the most significant was the abandoning of the principle that the civil society organizations would constitute a separate realm of the state, superior in status to the executive, legislature and judiciary. The system of 'social control' – which in some ways harked back to the principle of '*co-gobierno*' enunciated in 1952 and again at the time of the 1971 Popular Assembly – was thus seriously modified. In the event, the national electoral authority became a fourth power of the state. Social control in the new constitution was envisaged in various ways through greater participation in the procedures of policy-making. As we shall see, the new constitution enhanced women's and indigenous rights, affirmed the plural nature of the economy (with the state as an actor), and reaffirmed the control of the central government over land distribution issues.

The ways in which indigenous rights are protected and promoted under the new constitution are various. The text renamed the Republic of Bolivia as the Plurinational State of Bolivia, a formulation that emphasized the fact that the country is made up of different ethnicities or 'nations'. But perhaps most importantly, the new text envisaged a series of autonomies – departmental, municipal, regional and indigenous – which in part was designed to satisfy the aspirations of those in the *media luna* who had campaigned vociferously for greater autonomy while the text of the new constitution was debated. Indigenous autonomies, other than in their recognized territories (*Territorios Indígena Originario Campesinos*), were reduced to municipal level. As we shall see in the first chapter, the constitution also acknowledged other important areas of indigenous rights, including respect for bilingual education, the right of indigenous peoples to be consulted on issues affecting their livelihoods, respect for communitarian systems of justice, special rights to representation (though the number of indigenous deputies was reduced in the negotiations that followed the original draft text), and guarantees for communal forms of landholding where these exist. The final draft constitution was approved by a massive majority in the January 2009 referendum, held alongside a referendum on the maximum extension of landholding permissible.

While the passage of the new constitution – from the election of the Constituent Assembly in July 2006 through to its final approval in 2009 – proved contentious and problematic, the ways in which it would transform Bolivia and its political institutions would necessarily depend on how it was implemented through detailed legislation. Although the MAS won a majority in both chambers of the legislature in the 2009 elections, this was not the end of the story; the process of putting the constitution into effect was also to be hotly debated, and would be a hallmark of Evo's second administration beginning in January 2010. At the same time, the government was obliged to contend with a number of problems that sapped its popularity, undermined the unity on which it was elected, and opened up new opportunities for its adversaries to challenge its predominance over the country's politics. Two specific issues – the so-called *gasolinazo* of December 2010 and the dispute over building a road through the Territorio Indígena y Parque Nacional Isiboro Sécure (TIPNIS) – proved particularly corrosive. In spite of a relatively benign economic situation, the government found itself fighting off challenges from various quarters, including sectors that had previously been among its more stalwart supporters. Implementation of the constitution also proved more difficult than most had imagined at the outset, not least in terms of fulfilling the promises on indigenous rights contained in the new charter.

Conclusions

The election of Evo Morales brought to office a government which, unlike its predecessors, involved a wide range of social movements in the processes of government. This triggered a shift in the politics of *protesta* to those of *propuesta* and the implementation of public policy. As in the past, in 1952 and again in 1971, this involved awkward choices for those involved in social movements. Some sought to engage actively in the processes of government, especially those organically linked to the MAS. Others sought to maintain a distance from government, concerned that engagement would involve them in co-optation and the loss of their autonomy as social actors. At least during Morales's first period in government, such tensions were reduced as the process of writing a new constitution advanced, a constitution which all agreed was a historic necessity. But as time went on, the tensions became more pronounced. As we shall see in the first chapter, they became particularly acute in the rural sector with the breakdown of the Pacto de Unidad between different sectors of the campesino/indigenous movement. The Pact had provided the political understandings on which the formulation of the new constitution had been based. At the same time, rifts opened up in other areas, with the urban middle class increasingly restive over the policies adopted by the Morales administration. Still, at the end of 2012, the government enjoyed important organized support at the grassroots level, while its political opponents remained largely in disarray.

1 | LAND, CAMPESINOS AND *INDÍGENAS*

On 21 March 2011, twenty-one years to the day since the groundbreaking 1990 march by indigenous peoples of the eastern lowlands, a new march set out from Trinidad, the capital of the Beni, towards La Paz, 600 kilometres away. The VIII march, organized by the Confederación de Pueblos Indígenas de Bolivia (Cidob), was a protest march against government plans to construct a road through the Territorio Indígena y Parque Nacional Isiboro Sécure (TIPNIS). Like its forerunner, the VIII march was to have important ramifications, both nationally and internationally. It became a show of force of some sectors of Bolivia's indigenous peoples – highland as well as lowland – against a government policy that appeared to ignore indigenous demands and violate a constitutional commitment to organize prior consultations where indigenous lands or people are affected.

The TIPNIS – it is better known by its acronym – is a triangular piece of land of over a million hectares in the centre of Bolivia. Shaped like the head of a cat, it straddles the still-undefined border between the departments of Cochabamba to the south and Beni to the north. The area was declared a national park in 1965. In 2009, the Mojeño-Ignaciano, the Yuracaré and Chimán ethnic groups, which occupy the greater part of the area, were awarded title for their lands of the Territorio Indígena Originario Campesino (TIOC). The local indigenous population totalled some 12,000 people, mainly dependent on the forest and its natural produce. Carved out of the south of the national park is an area known as the Polígono 7, settled since the 1970s. It is now inhabited by up to 30,000 Aymara and Quechua-speaking migrants from the highlands, devoted largely to subsistence agriculture and a few cash crops like cocoa, bananas, citrus fruits and (significantly) coca. Polígono 7 abuts the Chapare district of Cochabamba, and the settlers form part of the Federación del Trópico, one of the six federations of coca growers of that region, of which Evo Morales is president.

Until fairly recently, the majority of Bolivians had probably never heard of the TIPNIS; it became a household name after the Morales government – without prior consultation (and indeed prior to the ratification of the new constitution) – signed a contract with a Brazilian construction firm to build a road through the centre of the reserve. This was the central section of a road project that would link Villa Tunari to the south (joining up with the Santa Cruz–Cochabamba trunk road) to San Ignacio de Moxos in the north (joining up with the dirt road from La Paz to Trinidad). Though several different routes had been mapped out, all crossed the TIPNIS. Alternative routes were either hobbled by the hilly terrain to the west or by marshy land to the east.

Part of the Amazon rainforest, the TIPNIS is an extraordinarily bio-diverse region, vulnerable to the sort of depredation that the rainforest has suffered elsewhere, particularly in Brazil. Most of its indigenous inhabitants live in settled communities, sixty-seven in total. However, some still live a nomadic lifestyle as hunter-gatherers. As well as land and timber, the TIPNIS area also includes probable hydrocarbon deposits, part of a belt stretching along the whole eastern flank of the Andes. Some prospection work has been carried out. The construction of a road through the TIPNIS would certainly lead to extensive deforestation, just as has been the case in Brazil. A study published by the PIEB (Programa de Investigaciones Estratégicas de Bolivia) suggests that over a period of twenty-five years, as much as 65 per cent of the present forest cover could be lost, not least because of the high market prices for hardwoods from the rainforest.

The road-building scheme quickly developed into conflict between those supporting it and those not. Arguments in favour included the positive impact a road would have on developing the country's road infrastructure, providing an important link between Cochabamba and the Beni. It was also seen as facilitating social development (education, health posts, etc.) in an area of extreme poverty where such services are largely absent. The road would also reduce the traditional economic dependence of the Beni on Santa Cruz. Those opposing the project pointed to the damaging consequences it would have for the environment, its negative impact on indigenous communities, and the spur it would provide to the northwards march of the *cocaleros* into new territory. Critics also pointed to the benefits that would accrue to Brazil, not to Bolivia, by providing a road link from Rondonia to the Pacific. The issue also raised questions of implementation of prior consultation, respect for indigenous lands and self-determination, key issues for indigenous people of the lowlands.

Attempts to broker an agreement for the project foundered on the lack of common ground: either a road is built or it is not. The issue soon became highly politicized, with the Cidob adding a number of other demands to its original opposition to the road, reflecting the interests of other ethnic groups who form part of the confederation. Internationally, the project swiftly became a cause célèbre, casting doubt on the indigenous and environmental credentials of the Morales administration. Destruction of the rainforest hardly squared with the official discourse of protecting the Pachamama (Mother Earth) and standing up for the interests of indigenous peoples. On the other hand, the government – with its close links to the *cocaleros* – was loath to have its agenda dictated to by a small minority of the population living in the reserve. The VIII march thus set off from Trinidad with neither side willing to back down and the government apparently committed to the road going ahead.

Visions of development

The TIPNIS dispute was to have lasting resonance in Bolivian politics, both for the immediate issues it raised and for the way it highlighted different visions of development. As we saw in the Introduction, various social movements, representing different sectors of the population, came together in 2003 around the October Agenda and, concretely, around the electoral campaign of the Movimiento al Socialismo (MAS) in 2005. The so-called Pacto de Unidad, agreed in 2004, brought together campesinos and indigenous peoples around a programmatic agreement: basically the rewriting of the constitution. The Pacto de Unidad included those who saw themselves as 'fundamental' to the establishment of the MAS as their 'political instrument', and those who saw themselves more loosely as 'allies'. The *'fundamentales'* included the peasant confederation (CSUTCB); the women's arm of the CSUTCB, the Confederación Bartolina Sisa (CNMCIOB-BS); and the confederation of *colonizadores*, which has renamed itself the Confederación de Comunidades Interculturales (CSCIB). They also, of course, included the coca farmers' federations of both the Yungas and the Chapare, both closely related to the Interculturales. The *'aliados'* consisted basically of the two indigenous confederations, the Cidob (representing lowland indigenous peoples) and Conamaq (Consejo Nacional de Ayllus y Markas del Qullasuyu, representing highland indigenous peoples organized in *ayllus*).

What united these various different sectors was the possibility of engineering a new deal of legal and constitutional rights for the large proportion of the Bolivian rural population that had always found itself excluded from the political class. In practice, 62 per cent of the population of Bolivia self-identified as 'belonging to some *originario* or indigenous peoples' in the 2001 census, making it a more 'indigenous' country than any other in Latin America. Despite the difficulty of defining 'indigenousness' in very precise terms, there had always been a large overlap between ethnicity and class in the country; the peasantry and working class were largely of indigenous extraction. The term 'campesino' tended to be used to describe the socio-economic status of rural communities, while the term 'indigenous' tended to refer to historic and cultural identities. Indeed, as Xavier Albó, an anthropologist, put it to us, in the Andean area as a whole, rural populations are referred to as 'indigenous campesinos' or, alternatively, as *'campesino indígenas'*. Still, between indigenous movements as such and those of the peasantry, there were (and are) important defining characteristics, relating to economic activity, but particularly to the ownership of land.

The 1953 agrarian reform was premised on the idea of individual landownership, with the division of hacienda lands among their former workers. Although peasant communities might embrace some communal landownership and decision-making might be collective, more productive land tended to be individually farmed and its produce individually marketed. This tradition permeated those who, as a result of land shortages in the Altiplano, migrated to the areas of colonization – both formal and informal – in other parts of the country, but particularly in the tropics of La Paz, Cochabamba and Santa Cruz. Individual landownership was not, however, the practice of indigenous groups in the eastern lowlands, whose traditions were often nomadic and not circumscribed by notions of landownership. In the Altiplano, too, despite the agrarian reform and its effects, age-old communitarian traditions of landownership persisted in the form of the *ayllu*, albeit often with individual possession and use of land. As we shall see in Chapter 2, the resurgence of indigenous consciousness in the highlands since the 1980s has led to attempts to reconstitute individually held land as collectively held, at least in those parts where such a tradition existed. The 1953 agrarian reform had, basically, sought to address landholding in the Altiplano and the inter-Andean valleys, where haciendas had predominated. The reform did not contemplate land distribution issues in lowland Bolivia, where traditionally land had been held in large units and where, in the 1960s, new forms of cash-crop agriculture emerged on large privately owned estates. The 1996 agrarian law, known as the INRA Law after the institution charged with carrying it out (the Instituto Nacional de Reforma Agraria), sought to address some of the inequities that had emerged in the meantime, particularly with regard to the rights of lowland indigenous communities. It introduced the concept of the Tierras Comunitarias de Orígen (TCO), based upon notions of collective ownership and territorial control. These two conceptions of landholding – individual and collective, peasant and 'indigenous' – have increasingly, as we shall see, proved uneasy bedfellows.

The TIPNIS dispute – and many others in recent times which have received far less publicity – involved conflicts over the nature of landholding. For indigenous groups, particularly those of the lowlands, the TCO was a very significant conquest, providing legal guarantees for a traditional way of life which had not been recognized by the 1953 agrarian legislation. The formation of the Cidob in 1982, first by ethnic groups from Santa Cruz and then subsequently from other lowland departments such as Beni, Pando and parts of Tarija, aimed to secure such guarantees. In essence it is a loose alliance, rather than a very formal structure. Among its original promoters were the Chiquitanos, one of the more numerous of the peoples of eastern Santa Cruz, whose lands had come under attack from the expansion of cash-crop agriculture. Other founder members included the Guarayos, Guaraníes and the Ayoreos. The Cidob gave rise to a number of smaller regional organizations dedicated to preserving indigenous rights in general, but land rights in particular. In some instances, such as among the Guaraní in southern Santa Cruz, indigenous groups were even prepared to buy the land they needed. For most indigenous groups territory has much more than just an economic meaning. It represents the guarantee of cultural and even spiritual survival. This was made very clear to us in the interviews we conducted with the Suyu Jatun Killaka Asanajaqi (Jakisa) in southern Oruro, a highland indigenous people who have sought to reassert their ethnic identity through the reconstitution of *ayllus*. For them, this is the reconquest of an identity suppressed since colonial times. According to Antonio Maraza, who presided over a meeting we attended, 'it's about decolonization and restoring ourselves as we used to be'. The introduction of the TCO therefore has a political dimension which implies a degree of decision-taking and self-determination, self-government (*autonomía*), the preservation of resources, and respect for traditional modes and customs (*usos y costumbres*) – not least regarding judicial matters. Collective ownership of land does not, however, imply collective forms of production; rather it means that land cannot be bought and sold as if it were a commodity. One of the criticisms frequently levelled at the peasant approach to landholding is that it is essentially 'mercantilist' in that its main objective is, through trade, to make money, even if at the expense of the rest of the community and the environment. José Bailaba, one of the founders of the Organización Indígena Chiquitana (OICh) in the eastern part of Santa Cruz, puts it thus: 'They have a different vision of things. For them there is no land that is respected as a reserve [...] their view is that looking after nature is a waste of time, a distraction from the business of making money.'

Indigenous organizations in the eastern lowlands were among those that pushed most consistently for the need to include such rights, based on land, in a new constitution. The 1990 march from Trinidad to La Paz proved highly influential, not least in paving the way to the 1996 Ley INRA. 'Before the march, no one took any notice of us,' says Bailaba; with it 'we emerged on the political stage'. Subsequent marches – these became a hallmark of indigenous mobilization – paved the way towards constitutional change. The III march in 2000 aimed to bring changes in the administration of the INRA Law, while the IV march in 2002 highlighted the need for a Constituent Assembly to change the constitution and thereby legally guarantee self-government and self-determination within indigenous territories. For Bailaba, the formation of the Pacto de Unidad had the sole purpose of passing the constitution. 'For us, it never had more permanence than that,' he says.

Campesino organizations take a rather different view, although there has been a good deal of overlap between peasant and indigenous demands in the past, and there are areas of Bolivia – Pando is a good example (see Chapter 8) – where indigenous and peasant organizations have worked harmoniously together, engaged in similar activities and usually in the face of a common enemy such as the *latifundista* or (in Pando) the *barraquero*. However, the problem of pressure on the land, both in the Altiplano and the valleys, has led to increasing hardship over the years as *minifundios* subdivide from one generation to the next into what are sometimes called '*surcofundios*', a single furrow of crops. Lorenzo Soliz, the national director of CIPCA, a rural development NGO with programmes in both the Altiplano and the lowlands, points out that with plots of 1–2 hectares, peasant families in the highlands are simply unable to support themselves. 'Is it surprising that they are demanding land?' he asks. The overflow of peasant populations into the tropics has often been at the expense of indigenous lands. This is the prime cause, for example, of the growing pressure on the land in the Chapare and in the Polígono 7, as well as in some of the areas to the north of Santa Cruz city, which were originally settled by *colonizadores* in the 1960s and 1970s. For Juan de Dios Fernández, the director of planning at INRA, it is also a problem of the scale of TCO awards to indigenous peoples, the relatively low numbers of people living in them, and the poor management of the land provided. 'They are unable to control the uses to which it is put,' he says, citing how some sell off or rent parts of TCOs to timber extraction companies. Lorenzo Soliz agrees: 'the challenge is how to manage this land', he says. Some Interculturales go as far as to say that the TCO/TIOC are the new *latifundios*.

Indigenous rights and the constitution

Disagreements between peasants and indigenous groups over landholding emerged as a powerful and highly politicized dispute only with the TIPNIS case in 2011. The Pacto de Unidad held together until then, by which time the new constitution had been ratified by referendum and had entered into force. As we shall see, many of these issues regarding landholding were not resolved one way or another in the constitutional document, and contradictions would dog its implementation. However, the 2009 constitution can be regarded in a very real sense as a political victory for indigenous movements in enshrining a number of important rights into law in ways which will not easily be reversed.

We have already alluded to the role of the various indigenous marches in the eastern lowlands as powerful impulses towards constitutional reform. The emergence of politically astute indigenous leaderships in the 1990s and 2000s and the building of influential forms of grassroots organization and coordinating mechanisms like the Cidob provided a crucial input into what became known, after 2003, as the 'October Agenda'. One of its key points was the need for a complete overhaul of the constitution. This dated from 1967 at the time of the military government of General René Barrientos, although it had been modified in some important respects during the Sánchez de Lozada government in the 1990s. The 1967 constitution updated the 1938 constitution, concocted behind closed doors with virtually no public participation. The process of devising the 2009 constitution was to be very different, with a great deal of participation and by groups which had traditionally played little or no part in the formal politics of the country.

The assembly which was elected in July 2006 to reform the constitution involved a wide array of people who had previously taken part in the social movements that flourished in the early part of the decade: peasants, indigenous people and representatives from urban neighbourhood organizations (*juntas vecinales*) and from organized trade unions. With a majority of members elected on the MAS ticket, it was presided over by Silvia Lazarte, a campesina from Villa Tunari in the Chapare. Lazarte had previously been a leader of the Bartolina Sisa, the women's peasant confederation. This was the first ever elected assembly in which campesinos and indigenous peoples were strongly represented. For many of those elected, their involvement in the Constituent Assembly was a highly educative process. Among others, the Cidob played an important role from 2006 onwards, helping to marshal ideas and lobbying behind the scenes in Sucre where the assembly was convened. 'It managed to influence decisions and even impose some [decisions] on the president himself,' says Leonardo Tamborini, the head of CEJIS, an NGO based in Santa Cruz with strong ties to the Cidob.

The document that was finally approved involved substantial advances in the area of indigenous rights. Perhaps the first and most obvious change was the re-establishment of Bolivia as a 'plurinational state', meaning that it is a state made up of indigenous 'nations' with rights to 'autonomy, self-government, culture, recognition of their institutions and the consolidation of their territorial entities' (Article 2). Article 30 of the constitution specifies a number of specific rights for indigenous peoples – eighteen in total. These include rights to collective land titling, respect for cultural symbols and values, access to education that is 'intracultural, intercultural and plurilingual', consultation in cases where they are affected by 'legislative or administrative decisions', and obligatory prior consultation with respect to 'exploitation of non-renewable natural resources on their territory', to participation in the benefits of exploiting such natural resources, and to the autonomous management of their territories. In addition, Article 31 commits the state to respecting and protecting 'indigenous nations and peoples in danger of extinction, in situations of voluntary isolation and [those] non-contacted'. In other respects, the constitution holds out special representative rights in the Chamber of Deputies for indigenous peoples, rights of communitarian justice according to '*usos y costumbres*', a regime of indigenous autonomous government; and the protection of collective land rights. The constitution (Article 8) also proclaims adherence to a number of indigenous ethical and moral principles, including that of *vivir bien*. This latter, which, as we will see, means rather different things to different peoples, is usually taken to mean living in harmony with the community and with the environment. Afrobolivians were accorded the same rights in the constitution as indigenous peoples.

The ratification of the new constitution was undoubtedly a major achievement in the area of extending rights to those who previously had few. This was acknowledged by almost all those we interviewed, but at the same time it would take real effect only once translated into detailed legislation and then implemented. This seemed to be the main task ahead as the second Morales administration took office at the beginning of 2010. Some legislation followed fairly swiftly on the promulgation of the constitution: a law regulating the electoral system (and in so doing creating special representation for rural indigenous minorities); a law of autonomies (among them indigenous autonomies); and a law establishing the parameters of communitarian justice in indigenous areas. The law of autonomies decentralizes certain powers to departmental, regional and municipal layers of government. Among these are eleven indigenous munici-palities, where government operates according to local custom. At the time of writing, a law on prior consultation was under discus-sion, although not before the whole issue had been sullied by the TIPNIS dispute. But as Gustavo Soto, from CEADESC, an NGO in Cochabamba, pointed out, the new constitution involved a number of inconsistencies and contradictions, not least with regard to in-digenous rights. He sees 'two irreconcilable aspects' of, on the one hand, respect for indigenous rights and the notion of *vivir bien*, and on the other maintenance of an economic model based on extractive industries and the generation of rents therefrom. The official line, however, enunciated by Vice-President Alvaro García Linera, was that the two elements had to be combined. The law on the Madre Tierra and Integral Development, passed in October 2012, stressed the importance of 'development' projects in bringing benefits to often remote indigenous communities in jungle areas like the TIPNIS, as well as the need for effective environmental protection. The problem so far as the latter was concerned was how to ensure environmental controls are enforced.

For many of the indigenous communities that had actively promoted the new constitution, these laws proved something of a disappointment. Indigenous representation was reduced to only seven seats in the chamber, fewer than indigenous groups had been led to believe. Though the law of autonomies set up indigenous autonomies, based on existing municipalities, many groups were not able to realize this objective because their lands straddled existing administrative boundaries. But perhaps more important, the promise of a 'plurinational state' proved difficult to put into practice. As Jorge Cortés at CEADESC puts it, 'there is no proper participation on the part of *pueblos indígenas* in the running of the state; where are the plurinational institutions?' He argues that 'it's ministers who have the last word, not *pueblos indígenas* [...] we need specific spaces for indigenous people in all institutions of the state'. Even at the grassroots level, tensions have emerged between the pretensions of TCOs (or TIOCs) as spaces in which indigenous peoples can make their own decisions and have them respected and the jurisdiction of a centralized state, particularly over the vexed issue of exploiting natural resources. How much of a say should local people have on such matters, and in what circumstances are such rights trumped by 'national' interests? This is a question which the constitution and the legislation stemming from it do not ultimately resolve.

Saneamiento, land titling and redistribution

In spite of the 1953 agrarian reform, Bolivia has been one of the Latin American countries with the greatest inequality of landholding. Notwithstanding its objectives of providing land for the landless, the policies stemming from the agrarian reform encouraged huge accumulations of land in the eastern half of the country, often at the expense of indigenous peoples living there. The Guaraní of the Chaco in southern Santa Cruz and the eastern part of Tarija were a case in point, ending up as slave-like indentured labourers on privately owned estates. The biggest beneficiaries of the land reform programme turned out in the long term to be large-scale private agricultural enterprise and medium-sized landowners, while in the legislation there was no recognition of the needs of indigenous peoples as such. The 1996 INRA reform sought, in part, to deal with this problem by defining the territories demanded by indigenous peoples and setting the boundaries of privately owned properties within them (*saneamiento*) and introducing systems of land titling. The concept of the TCO was developed as a means of giving legal protection to indigenous peoples living on collectively owned (and often very large) tracts of land. Both peasant and indigenous organizations had demanded a new law; and indeed the 1990 march by indigenous peoples of the Oriente had demanded *saneamiento* of landholding and the confirmation of land rights. In 2006, shortly after it took office, the Morales administration introduced some changes to the existing Ley INRA in order to speed up the process of *saneamiento* and titling while tackling some of the more blatant inequities in patterns of land redistribution.

The process of *saneamiento* did indeed speed up. The original law specified that *saneamiento* had to be complete within ten years, but at the end of this period, in 2006, only around 10 per cent had been achieved. According to official figures, the total amount of land *saneado* and titled in this period was 9.3 million hectares. From 2006 to 2011 the amount increased fivefold to 51.7 million hectares. The cost of *saneamiento* was also cut dramatically, by avoiding the use of foreign consultants, from US$10 a hectare to US$1.60. So the total area affected by 2011 was 57.2 per cent. The total amount of land affected by the Ley INRA between 1996 and 2010 was roughly the same as had been covered by the agrarian reform over the previous forty years. Of the area *saneado* and titled between 1996 and 2011, 23.2 million hectares were defined as belonging to TCOs and roughly the same declared to be '*tierras fiscales*'. *Tierras fiscales* are lands in the hands of the state which can then be redistributed to peasants and others in need of land. Whereas previously companies had benefited, during this period it was indigenous people and campesinos who got preference. Almost all the TCOs instituted between 1996 and 2005 were located in the lowlands of the east; after 2005, TCOs with collective property rights were also declared in the western highlands, to the benefit of indigenous groups there, as well as in the east. Some of the TCOs in the highlands covered huge areas with very sparse populations; in the south of Potosí, for example, there was one covering 3million hectares. The department in which the process of *saneamiento* and titling went farthest was Pando in the far north, where 100 per cent of the land susceptible to *saneamiento* had been covered by 2009. Much of the land there was declared to be *tierras fiscales* (where it was deemed not to fulfil a productive or social function) and then redistributed to peasant and indigenous peoples in the form of TCOs.

In terms of beneficiaries, the official figures show a total of around 800,000 individuals, particularly campesinos and indigenous people. Under the 2006 legislation, women's rights to hold land titles were enhanced, either as sole proprietors or jointly with their husbands. Of those awarded titles, 81 per cent were in joint names between husband and wife. The recognition of women's title to land represented an important break with past practice, significantly enhancing the status of campesino women.

The acceleration of the *saneamiento* programme owed a lot to a small group in charge at the INRA, led by Alejandro Almaraz, the vice-minister responsible for agrarian issues. In 2010, this team was dismantled. The speed of *saneamiento* slowed in 2011, with a total of 6 million hectares *saneado*, compared with an initial target for the year of 15 million. The 2006 law fixed 2013 as the target date for completing *saneamiento*, a target which in 2012 seemed impossible to achieve. For his part, Juan Carlos Rojas, who administered the programme of *saneamiento* between 2006 and 2010, sees a lack of commitment at the top to continuing with it. 'My big worry is that the cycle has ended,' he says, pointing to what he saw as a modus vivendi being established between the MAS government and large private landowners. He also sees the fall-off in impetus as resulting from pressure on the government by the peasant confederation (CSUTCB) to call a halt to the creation of new TCOs. The CSUTCB was pressing the government in 2011 and 2012 for a new Land Law which might offer a return to individual landholdings.

Rojas also points to the opposition from large landowners to the programme of enhanced land reform espoused by the INRA after 2006. Indeed, this was one of the main reasons why the programme after 1996 achieved disappointing results. 'They [large landowners] act to defend their interests,' he says. Juan de Díos Fernández, the director of planning at the INRA, agrees, pointing to the example of the way in which the political elite of Santa Cruz targeted the INRA office in the city, as well as in Trinidad (in the Beni) and Cobija (in Pando) during the disturbances of September 2008, when offices were ransacked and documents relating to land tenure decisions stolen. According to Rojas, the objective of the INRA was to redistribute land, 'taking it away from medium and large-scale farmers and giving it to campesinos and *indígenas*' by nationalizing land not being productively used and turning it into *tierras fiscales* for subsequent redistribution. 'But to do that you have to go through the process of *saneamiento* first,' he says. He claims that 10 million hectares were acquired in this way, of which 4 million were distributed to campesinos, mostly in Pando, Beni, northern La Paz, the Chaco and Santa Cruz.

As a result of this land programme, rural incomes appear to have risen. This has been more the case in the lowlands than in the highlands, according to Lorenzo Soliz at CIPCA. 'The fact that people have more land means a lot,' he says; 'not only do they have greater productive capacity but they have greater power of negotiation.' Another of the positive social achievements of *saneamiento* also appears to have been the elimination of debt peonage (*servidumbre*) on some private landed estates in parts of eastern Bolivia. 'We proved it still existed,' says Rojas. 'Now some landowners have even registered their workers with the Caja' (for health insurance purposes), he says.

Breakdown of the Pacto

As we saw in the Introduction, one of the salient features of rural politics in Bolivia over the past twenty years has been the increase in levels of organization and the degree of empowerment of both peasants and those who belong to specific ethnic groups. It was in the 1980s that the CSUTCB and its affiliate organizations challenged the sort of clientelistic politics that typified the MNR and military regimes of the preceding period. The 1990 march of the indigenous peoples of the Oriente then signalled the coming of age of the ethnic groups of the lowlands and the awakening of pro-indigenous movements in the highlands with the formation of the Conamaq. In 2004 the Pacto de Unidad brought together these two traditions around discussion and lobbying on common issues. It represented a strong political underpinning for the MAS as it developed as an alternative to the status quo in the first years of the new millennium. However, as we have seen, the Pacto began to unravel from 2009 with the ratification of the new constitution. The rift became deeper, and possibly more permanent, with the VIII march of lowland indigenous peoples protesting at the government's plans for road-building in the TIPNIS.

With the VIII march, the power of indigenous peoples of the east reached a peak. The organizers of the march, basically the Cidob, forced the government into a U-turn on the road project, with the latter declaring the whole TIPNIS area as 'untouchable' (*intangible*) and cancelling the road project. The term '*intangible*' could be taken to mean preventing all economic activity in the TIPNIS, not something the indigenous population wanted; as such the decision did little to improve relations. With a strong show of unity among its component organizations (not always noted for their common positions), through the VIII march the Cidob showed it could mobilize opinion far beyond the confines of its own support base. For a start, it was backed by an important part of Conamaq, which was increasingly in conflict with the CSUTCB over extending its support base in the highlands. The marchers also received the sympathy of significant parts of the urban population, especially on their arrival in October 2011 in the city of La Paz. The influence of the march was amplified by the attention given to it in the media as it advanced day by day over two months through the tropics of the Beni and La Paz, finally crossing the cordillera to reach the seat of government. Opposition politicians and groups began to sense an opportunity to claw back lost political support by expressing their solidarity with the Cidob and its aims. The TIPNIS march also had major resonance at the international level, showing Evo Morales as less than consistent at home in his global appeal for respect for indigenous peoples and for the safeguarding of the Pachamama, or Mother Earth.

However, not all indigenous people living in or close to the TIPNIS were so keen on stopping the road. Those living in Polígono 7, organized as CONISUR, with closer links to the government, mounted a counter-march, enabling the government to backtrack once again, gaining the promise of a *consulta* on the issue among the groups affected. Such a consultation would be, as the Cidob was quick to point out, hardly 'prior' (as recommended by the ILO Convention 167) nor, in all probability, 'in good faith'.

The IX march, which again set out from Trinidad in April 2012, sought to reaffirm the determination to stop the road; it also sought to block the government's plans for a *consulta*. However, the IX march was not to be the conspicuous success for its organizers that the VIII march had been. Taking advantage of the situation, the government was far more proactive in seeking to undermine support for the leaders of the march than it had been the previous year. It also managed to besmirch the reputation of Cidob and its leaders, not least because of the agreements reached between them and some members of the conservative political elite in Santa Cruz. The IX march ended, having reached La Paz, empty handed, with its leaders under question. The recriminations within the Cidob and its organizations effectively divided the indigenous movement into two mutually antagonistic camps, the government clearly supporting those favouring the building of the road.

But behind these events, the policies of the Morales government on agrarian issues appeared to have shifted away from the agenda it had pursued in the period since 2006. Those who had designed and implemented the policies of *saneamiento* and land titling were removed from office, including Almaraz and Rojas. The rhythm of the INRA's programme of *saneamiento* slowed, and no new TCOs were declared. The CSUTCB became more assertive, preparing new proposals for legislation on land issues. And in a meeting between the government and social movements that took place in Cocha-bamba at the end of 2011, at which the Cidob was not present but the confederation of private businessmen was, it was mooted that the rules on supervising *latifundio* estates for compliance with the rules on productive use should be relaxed, with inspections every five years, not two. But the shift had probably begun before this, in the wake of the disturbances of 2008, which led to a gradual accommodation between the MAS government and the agribusi-ness elites of the Oriente. In January 2009, at the same time as the ratification of the constitution, there had been a referendum on the upward limit on privately owned estates, an issue on which the Constituent Assembly had failed to find agreement. Voters ended up approving a 5,000-hectare upper limit (the lower of the two op-tions presented) but – significantly – the limit would not be made retroactive. Those in Santa Cruz and the Beni who had accumulated units of landholding far in excess of this limit were much relieved.

The reasons for and the extent of this change in policy still remained somewhat unclear at the time of writing. One possible explanation was political, in the sense that the government sought to avoid the sort of political showdown that had occurred in September 2008 through a strategy of isolating the political elite in Santa Cruz from its erstwhile business backers. The confrontation brought Bolivia close to territorial rupture. By providing businessmen with guarantees, particularly over the vexed issue of land, the government managed to open up a space for dialogue with the *cruceño* elite, even if failing to convince it at an ideological level. The second hypothesis is more economic than political. Just as the business elite realized that the insurrectionary strategy was a non-starter and that there was no option but to engage with the government and negotiate policies that favoured its interests, it became clear to the government that Santa Cruz was effectively the country's breadbasket; if it wished to guarantee supplies of food to an increasingly urban population, it would need to maintain an 'open doors' policy towards agribusiness, since (as we shall see in Chapter 7) this had come to play a key role in providing both food for the domestic market and cash crops (like soya) for export.

The ramifications here for relations between peasants, indigenous groupings and large-scale agricultural producers remained unclear for the longer term. However, the demands of the 'productive' revolution appeared to have trumped those of the 'agrarian' revolution (land reform), to which the MAS government had given its support in its early days. Although with the breakdown of the Pacto de Unidad peasant producers and indigenous groups increasingly sang from different hymn sheets, their interests were hardly aligned with producers of cash crops (like soya and sunflower) and their industrialist partners. The sources of conflict within the rural sphere in Bolivia thus remained a threat to long-term political stability, particularly regarding landholding.

Conclusions

The first Morales administration involved a new deal for indigenous peoples in Bolivia. As a result of the speeding up of the programme of *saneamiento*, the number of TCOs and the area designated as such was greatly increased. The 2009 constitution led to the expansion of indigenous rights; indeed, the process by which the constitution was formulated involved an unprecedented degree of participation by campesinos and *indígenas*, working together under the Pacto de Unidad. However, ultimately a constitution is but a piece of paper, and its real impact would become evident only in the years that followed. It would require detailed legislation in a multiplicity of spheres to put into effect the 411 articles included in the constitution. And that legislation would need to be implemented and enforced in order for the full effect of the constitution to be measured. As of 2012, it was far too early to assess its full impact, its achievements and its limitations. While some of the legislation had been placed on the statute book and efforts were under way to push ahead with implementation, there was increasing dissatisfaction about the way in which indigenous rights were being applied in practice.

What had emerged by 2012, however, were very different understandings of development on the part of indigenous peoples on the one hand and campesinos on the other, with notions of economic 'progress' and 'development' clashing with those of environmentalism and '*vivir bien*', notions that even conflicted with one another within rural communities. This was dramatized by the TIPNIS dispute, but there were other instances too. It is important to remind ourselves here that, historically, the distinction between what was 'indigenous' and what was 'campesino' had been far from clear cut; most campesinos were indigenous and most indigenous people were campesinos. But what the TIPNIS showed was that there were differences in the nature of landholding stemming, on the one hand, from the 1953 agrarian reform, and on the other from the 1996 INRA Law. While the expansion of indigenous rights contained in the constitution helped reinforce the claims of those whose lands were held in collective form (both in the highlands and the lowlands) and whose culture and distinctiveness had been denied by the 1953 agrarian reform, it did less for the campesino for whom the problem of land shortage had never been properly resolved by the 1953 reform. Indeed, as we have seen, the Morales government failed to provide a solution for a sector of the population which is its main political ally, whose main remedy for land shortage in the past had been migration, to the lowlands, the cities and abroad. While the

Morales government had taken up the standard of indigenous rights, the issue of paucity of land suitable for agricultural development in the Altiplano was the reality with which the president had grown up and knew from personal experience.

The gaining of titles to land for some 800,000 people (both campesinos and *indígenas*) has been of fundamental importance in the lives of the beneficiaries of land titling, who represent almost a tenth part of the country's population. In particular, the ability of women to own land constitutes an important step forward. This is empowerment in a very real and concrete form and, as Lorenzo Soliz at CIPCA made clear to us, land redistribution on this scale has an important bearing on poverty reduction. The achievements of land distribution in recent years have perhaps been the single most important contribution to social inclusion. However, the process of redistribution of land has largely left untouched the larger landowners. If the owner of the few furrows of land in the Altiplano is to make enough to live on, inequalities in land redistribution will have to be properly addressed. With different views emerging among campesinos and indigenous people regarding the nature of landholding, however, the question of further land redistribution still lies in the balance.

The need for further land redistribution, however, seems to be at odds with the need to produce food for an increasingly urbanized population, for which the immediate priority is to secure food at competitive prices for the ever-increasing sector of the population not involved in agriculture. With a large proportion of food needs being met by large-scale agribusiness, mainly in Santa Cruz, this implied forging a new relationship with such producers, something that does not necessarily augur well for the peasant producers who had been among the government's most stalwart supporters.

This chapter perhaps poses more questions than it answers. Can protection of Mother Earth and 'development' be reconciled with one another? How much of a say should/can people have when development in the national interest affects their lands? What alternatives does a government of the poorest country in the Latin American region actually have with large numbers of its population still living in poverty? Can the needs of rural producers be meshed with those of an increasingly urban society where cheap food is a necessity? Can a more equitable system of landholding be reconciled with the need for agribusiness? The Morales government in Bolivia finds itself wrestling with these problems; it has not necessarily come up with all the answers.

2 | THE ALTIPLANO: *SINDICATOS* VERSUS *AYLLUS*

The high plains of Bolivia, the Altiplano, stretch from east to west, separating the rims of the Andes mountain chain. The eye can see for ever in this vast, largely treeless landscape, broken only occasionally by small communities. On top of the world, the deep blue skies give way to a myriad of subtle colours: purples, pinks and blues in the distance, the burnt gold and dusty greens of the grasses. The snowy peaks of Andean mythology – Illimani, Illampu, Sajama – bear testimony to the retreat of their glaciers with the temperature increases over recent decades. The big lakes like the Titicaca to the north reflect every colour of blue, green and grey. The immense shimmering white salt lake of Uyuni, a key tourist attraction, stretches out southwards into Potosí.

The Altiplano is close to 4,000 metres above sea level. It is where, since pre-Columbian times, a large proportion of the rural population has eked out a precarious living from the land. Its agricultural potential is limited to the production of a small range of crops, of which the countless varieties of potato have loomed large. It is also an area where llamas and sheep are raised. Until recently, it has been a major area for food production. Its climate is often harsh, subject to drought, storms and frosts, and the quality of much of the land is poor. However, it is a part of Bolivia where much of the country's rural population has traditionally resided, often in contexts of extreme poverty.

Agrarian reform and beyond

Until the 1950s, most of the land – certainly most of the productive land – was held in large privately owned haciendas that exploited a semi-servile labour force. According to the 1950 census, more than 70 per cent of the population of Bolivia was rural, based predominantly in the Altiplano departments of La Paz, Oruro and Potosí and the more fertile Andean valley regions to the east, especially around Cochabamba, Sucre and Tarija. While these areas provided food for the relatively small urban population and for the mining communities in the highlands, peasant communities living on the margins of hacienda land were largely involved in subsistence agriculture.

Pressure to change this system of landholding had built up in the 1940s, particularly in the valley of Cochabamba, which saw frequent land invasions of haciendas by peasants. Not only was the structure of landholding socially unjust, it was highly inefficient economically. Before 1952, around 5 per cent of landholders owned 90 per cent of cultivable land, one of the most unequal systems of landholding anywhere in Latin America. And most haciendas used only a small fraction of their extensive lands for agricultural purposes.

The 1952 revolution was the *coup de grâce* for the old, quasi-feudal systems of land tenure. It brought to an end, at least in principle, the use of servile labour. It ushered in a radical redistribution of land, officialized by the August 1953 agrarian reform. Although the main motor for agrarian change did not come from the Altiplano, the haciendas that had dominated the agricultural landscape were divided up, to the benefit of the populations that worked in them in one form or another. Those that remained saw their landholding reduced dramatically.

The agrarian reform gave way to a system of small-scale production in *minifundios*, organized around peasant communities that resembled the traditional indigenous *ayllus* but which were organized as agrarian *sindicatos* by the governments at the time. The peasant population, both of the valleys and the Altiplano, became one of the key social props of the MNR and the military regimes that followed. The official discourse spoke of campesinos, not indigenous people, though, as we suggested in Chapter 1, most campesinos are indigenous. The problem of division of the land into ever smaller parcels – sometimes referred to as *surcofundios* (a *surco* being a single furrow of crops) – gave rise to the policy of colonization pursued from the late 1950s onwards. This led to the migration of some 70,000 peasant families from the Altiplano to settle the subtropical regions of the country, hitherto underpopulated, in the lowlands of La Paz, Cochabamba and Santa Cruz departments.

But these policies did little to improve matters for those who remained as small-scale producers in the Altiplano, producing in part for a growing urban market but also – in large measure – for their own subsistence. Lacking access to capital, faced with government policies that favoured agribusiness, and poorly positioned to assert themselves in the market for food, they remained – depending on the area – among the poorest of the poor in post-1952 Bolivia. Increases in population from generation to generation led to ever-increased subdivision of the available land, although migration – to the lowlands, to the cities (such as La Paz and El Alto) or to foreign countries (particularly Argentina) – provided something of a safety valve. The agrarian reform did little to resolve the dichotomy between *minifundios* and *latifundios*, since the 1960s and 1970s saw the growth of massive privately owned landed estates in the lowlands of Bolivia, particularly in the departments of Santa Cruz and the Beni.

By the late 1970s, new movements were afoot in the Altiplano that strove to break free of the domination of the peasant movement by the MNR and the military. The Kataristas, who included campesino leaders and young Aymaran intellectuals, began to mobilize not just around the issue of class but also of ethnicity. Independent peasant unions rallied round the Confederación Sindical Unica de Trabajadores Campesinos de Bolivia (CSUTCB), under the leadership of Jenaro Flores, the main campesino leader of the time. They had their roots in the Altiplano, but soon became an important force nationally. The CSUTCB gained a significant position within the popular movement, particularly following the closure of the state-owned mines, and the sacking of 27,000 mineworkers.

Amid the liberal reforms of the Sánchez de Lozada government was the attempt to regulate landownership through policies of land titling and *saneamiento*. The Ley INRA of 1996 set out a timetable for *saneamiento*, promising to complete the process within ten years. In practice, as we have seen, it managed to title barely 10 per cent of what it originally proposed in its first ten years of existence. Naturally, many of the large-scale *latifundios* in the lowlands rejected attempts to set legal limits to what they 'owned'. Among the main beneficiaries of the 1996 law were the lowland indigenous peoples, who gained legal status as Tierras Comunitarias de Origen (TCOs). But for the peasants of the Altiplano, the Ley INRA brought scant benefit. For them the problem was not one of land titling but the inability to sustain themselves on ever-decreasing areas of land, caught as they were in a cycle of declining productivity and income.

Of *ayllus* and *sindicatos*

It was in a small backyard in the small town of Challapata, situated between Oruro and Uyuni, that in 1997 a new confederation was established to represent and promote the interests of highland indigenous organizations, the Consejo Nacional de Ayllus y Markas del Qullasuyu (Conamaq). The dynamic behind the reconstitution of peasant organization along the lines of historic institutions, such as *ayllus* and *markas*, went back to the 1980s. In 1988, for example, precisely in the area of Challapata, the Federación de Ayllus del Sur de Oruro had been set up to this end. In 1997, this organization reconstituted itself as the Jatun Killaka Asanajaqi (suyu), bringing together the peoples of the Killaka nation. Reconstitution was also stimulated by the Ley INRA, with the stress it placed on the recognition by the state of the '*territorios*' of indigenous peoples, the TCOs as they were officially termed – commonly held land – as opposed to the '*tierra*' conceded under the earlier agrarian legislation to individual peasant families and their communities. The Ley INRA was given a new impulse by the Morales administration in 2006. Faced with strong pressure from campesino and indigenous sectors early in his government, Morales passed a law prolonging the process of *saneamiento* and clarifying some of its main points.

In practice, the reconstitution of *ayllus* in the Altiplano was far from straightforward. The notion of the *ayllu* involved the communal ownership of land, with families usually assigned plots in different areas of production, worked on a rotational basis. In much of the Altiplano, however, at least part of the land had long been in the hands of individual peasant families with only a proportion of land owned communally. The reconstitution of *ayllus*, recognized as TCOs by the state, therefore involved individually owned plots of land being renounced in favour of collective ownership. Not all members of the community were happy to give up their individual title to the land they had held. Reconstitution also involved the winding up of *sindicatos* in favour of *ayllus*. In many places this has caused a good deal of disagreement and conflict. According to the authorities of Jakisa, whose meeting we attended in the very same yard in Challapata, in the area reconstituted as *ayllus* 'there were *sindicatos* in some places, but not in others' and there were 'union leaders [*dirigentes sindicales*], general secretaries and *sub-centrales*', institutions typical of the old agrarian syndicates. The restitution of traditional institutions was not always welcome. Rivalries have sometimes turned violent, as in the cases of Norte Potosí and Coroma (on the border between Potosí and Oruro) in 2012.

The creation of TCOs (or TIOCs as they are now known) in the Altiplano dates almost entirely from the change of government in 2006. Previously, the process of land titling and *saneamiento* carried out under the auspices of the Ley INRA had concentrated on the lowlands of Bolivia. Most of the new highland TCOs were located in the southern part of the Altiplano, in the departments of Oruro, Potosí and the southern fringes of La Paz. The reasons why communities have opted to reconstitute the *ayllus* are various, but three in particular stand out.

First, it is a matter of cultural affirmation among Aymara and Quechua peoples of their rights as ethnic peoples to ancestral territories, often covering large tracts of land. The Jakisa authorities we met stressed the way in which their traditional customs and way of life were being eroded by the process of 'Westernization'. In the words of Antonio Maraza, who chaired the meeting in his traditional garb and with the insignia of his office, 'they introduce different languages, music and ways of dancing [...] We are forgetting our heritage, our designs, we are becoming lazy.' Several of the Jakisa authorities stressed how the 'Western' system of government had relegated them in the past, and how their cultural values were constantly under attack. 'They have introduced a different system of education,' says Antonio; 'the priests have us kneel down before them.' The problem of colonization is highly relevant for the Killaka and people like them. 'The Killaka people have not been recognized as a valid political structure by the state,' says Rudi Huayllas, who has worked alongside the Jakisa and is a member of the Killaka community. 'Colonialism involved us being assimilated as a population.'

For the authorities present at the meeting, the rights to territory formed part of a long-term project to reunite the Killaka people, dispersed throughout south-western Bolivia. The Jakisa as currently constituted consists of fourteen *markas* and seventy-four *ayllus*. But according to Antonio, there is 'still much to be done' to bring in those in Potosí and other departments. 'In pre-Inca times, our territory stretched into Argentina and Chile,' he maintains.

Secondly, the reconstitution of *ayllus* often greatly increased the amount of land available to communities, offering them also access to other resources. Whereas to be a campesino involved rights to land, to be an *indígena* involved rights to territory and to the resources to be found on (or under) it. 'Before [the creation of TCOs] our land was very limited,' argues Antonio Maraza. 'With collectively owned property, we have gained access to other forms of wealth.' This, in certain places, could mean access to mineral resources. According to Rudy Huayllas, under previous governments private firms managed to gain concessions for mining and quarrying, and members of communities found themselves having to pay for these resources. The claims of indigenous peoples to mineral reserves on their territory underlay some of the conflicts that emerged between communities and mining companies during the Morales administration. 'The INRA was helpful here,' Huayllas argues, in helping them regain control over territory. For his mother, it means having 40 hectares of land instead of 10.

Thirdly, TCOs can govern themselves autonomously and practise self-determination over a wide area of competences. This in fact is the challenge that indigenous peoples are facing: how to manage the areas under their responsibility.

Conamaq and the *ayllus* and *markas* affiliated to it broadly supported the Morales administration's efforts to reformulate the constitution and to incorporate within it an interpretation of indigenous rights. A key element here was the inclusion of a new notion of indigenous autonomy which complements the territoriality of the TCO. At the time of writing, eleven municipalities had decided to create indigenous autonomies (with more possibly in the pipeline), pending the approval of statutes of autonomy in line with the new constitution. In practice, indigenous autonomy represents three key principles: first, the election of authorities on the basis of time-honoured methods and procedures (*usos y costumbres*); second, the ability to manage the range of resources within territorial limits; and third, the ability to promulgate laws and regulations governing that territory, as well as to administer certain areas of justice within it. However, the extent to which real autonomy within the *ayllu* structure would be conceded is limited, since under the constitution control over non-renewable resources remains in the hands of the state.

While the restoration of *ayllus* and *markas* is seen as a historic conquest by those involved, it was by no means universal in its appeal. For many communities, it caused more problems than it resolved, particularly for those communities most dependent on *minifundista* agriculture for their livelihood, or where there was only limited access to extra land. It is notable, for example, that there was less interest in forming TCOs in much of the Altiplano in the department of La Paz, by contrast with the experience farther south, in Oruro and Potosí. In the northern Altiplano, since the time of the agrarian reform in the 1950s, land that was previously owned by haciendas was subdivided into small family plots. This has traditionally been one of the heartlands of peasant *sindicalismo*, and a bastion of the CSUTCB. The emergence of Conamaq in the late 1990s was a direct political challenge to the hegemony of the CSUTCB. Adherence to the traditions of agrarian *sindicatos* is more in evidence around the area of Lake Titicaca in the department of La Paz, though even here there have been attempts to reconstitute *ayllus*, and *sindicalismo* has adopted some of the trappings of indigenous culture. In Jesús de Machaca, close to the southern shore of the lake and one of the communities that has gone farthest down the road towards indigenous autonomy, it has proved difficult to do away with privately owned land.

Huarina, in the province of Omasuyos, for example, is a lakeside community relatively close to La Paz and El Alto, where there has been talk of reconstituting as an *ayllu* but no final decision had been made to do so. This was formerly a hacienda, belonging to a family called Meave. This had land in Huarina and surrounding areas, including an island in Lake Titicaca. With the agrarian reform the land was split up into plots owned by former hacienda labourers. Plots were small, varying in size from 1 to 8 hectares, though some of the land was also held in common. The local *sindicato agrario*, which dates from 1956, formed part of the hierarchy of union structures stretching up from the local to the national level. This historical longevity appears to be one reason why local people prefer to belong to an agrarian union structure rather than to an indigenous one like Conamaq. Though they have their criticisms of the way the CSUTCB works at present, the leaders of Conamaq are seen to be 'on the make' and not to have their interests at heart. However, the influence of *indigenismo* is clear, and the authorities we met in Huarina all adopted traditional forms of dress and carried the insignia of their office. They also referred to themselves as '*campesinos originarios*', rather than just plain campesinos. The influence of Felipe Quispe, the self-styled '*mallku*' (leader) of the Aymaran people and former leader of the CSUTCB, is clear in this part of Omasuyos, the province where he held most sway. 'He had the ability to mobilize,' said one of those we interviewed. Quispe comes from neighbouring Achacachi, which is historically known for its strong combative campesino leadership.

Ancoraimes is farther from La Paz, beyond Achacachi, but likewise close to the shores of Lake Titicaca. It is noted for the relative strength of its peasant organization, both historically and currently. In part, that organization was derived from the presence of the Methodist and Catholic churches in the area, influential in training local peasant leaders. The fifty-six communities within the municipality of Ancoraimes spread out from the lake, leading to the upper valleys and across the cordillera to those that give way to the subtropical Yungas. The dominance of rural communities over urban ones is more pronounced in Ancoraimes than in other municipalities in the Titicaca basin, and indeed the rural syndicates there exercise strong political influence over the affairs of the municipality. As in Huarina, Felipe Quispe was an influential figure, although people in Ancoraimes are reluctant to take their political cue from Achacachi. Iskaya is a small community on the shores of the lake, an hour from Ancoraimes by foot. Separated by steep hills from the surrounding area, it was never part of a hacienda. It has little land, most of it dedicated to crops, though community members also sell fish they catch from the lake. According to Jhonny Castillo Mamani, one of the younger community leaders, 'from one generation to the next we are dividing up the land like slices of cheese'. Iskaya has a *sindicato* that is affiliated to the CSUTCB. While critical of some aspects of the CSUTCB, the community leaders assured us that they participate in the affairs of the confederation at the local level. 'When we are called upon, we turn out,' says Feliciano López Mamani, one of the older members of the community. Jhonny Castillo adds that 'when there are conflicts, the leaders come down from the cantonal level, to the sub-central, and to the local level to mobilize people'. When asked whether they were considering affiliating to some other organization, he commented that they were not.

So how effective are these social organizations, linked to structures that ascend to national level, in articulating the needs of ordinary people in the Altiplano? The answers are necessarily mixed, depending on who you ask and where you go. Our interviews suggested that the process of reconstitution of *ayllus* and *markas* involved a questioning of the role traditionally played by the *sindicato*, a role viewed by some as suppressing the indigenous identity of highland peasants and integrating them into structures of state power dominated historically by the MNR.

The roles of each type of organization have traditionally been different. The agrarian trade union takes the demands of its grassroots members through local, regional structures to national level and puts political pressure on government to achieve change. The *ayllus*, meanwhile, have mainly had three functions: to protect their territorial boundaries, to plan and supervise food production, and to dispense community justice. Thus, the *ayllu* has tended to govern inwards, while the *sindicato* has played a more proactive political role beyond the community. In recent years, however, Conamaq and its regional organizations have begun to assume some of the outwardly more political functions of the *sindicato*.

For the *mallkus* we met in Challapata, who represented a number of *ayllus* in southern Oruro, the foundation of Conamaq represented the establishment of a new sort of social organization at national level. The various mobilizations in which they had been involved since then, particularly in 2002 and 2003, stood out in their memory as milestones in the development of their organization. However, they also recognized that, although they had established a degree of influence in regional politics, their decision-making ability was still strictly limited. They also recognized that their capacity to act not just as *ayllus* but as a 'nation' was limited because of the administrative and political boundaries – particularly between the departments of Oruro and Potosí (between which there are some deeply rooted conflicts over land and natural resources) – cut across traditional boundaries of ethnicity. Bonds of solidarity between the Killakas appeared to strengthen communal organization and to encourage unity of purpose. And the emphasis given to traditional *usos y costumbres* was such as to legitimize leadership through the practice of rotation of authorities, in this case every two years. Still, as Antonio Maraza admitted, 'our organization is still weak'. And, as Rudy Huayllas made clear, the restitution of traditional forms of landholding and community governance did not preclude conflict, particularly in terms of access to the most productive land. This has become a pressing problem in areas of production of quinua, one of the few crops on the Altiplano for which prices have boomed in recent years.

Farther north, around Lake Titicaca where *sindicatos* still prevail, people appeared to be more questioning of organizational structures and their efficacy, notably the CSUTCB. In recent years, a growing breach seems to have developed between union leaders and their membership. The memory of the mobilizations that took place prior to 2006, in which communities took part en masse, appeared to have faded, and they felt that the election of the MAS government had led to a degree of demobilization. Around both Ancoraimes and Huarina, community organization had become notably more lax. Whereas previously communities and their leaders had met regularly to discuss issues of mutual interest, the frequency of such meetings was now much more intermittent. In the community of Iskaya, for instance, whereas community meetings had been held once a month, or sometimes even fortnightly, they were now held only twice a year. Also, involvement in the affairs of the CSUTCB was less than before. As Joaquín Castillo, one of the older members of the community, put it: 'As a grassroots organization, we feel excluded. We take part in marches, but they fine us thirty bolivianos if we do not.' In Huarina, community leaders were critical of the leadership of the CSUTCB, accusing both this and the COB of being unwilling to fight for higher agricultural prices that would benefit producers like them.

One of the key reasons for the weakening of grassroots-level organization across the Altiplano is the migration of community members to the city, particularly to El Alto. One of the features of many communities in the Altiplano is the growing proportion of older people who are left in the communities. The younger and more dynamic members seek to augment their otherwise meagre incomes by working in the urban environment for most of the time, returning to their communities intermittently, for example for fiestas and other community events. The nearer the community to the city, the greater the proportion who tend to migrate. In the communities around Huarina, only some fifty kilometres from El Alto, most of the permanent residents tend to be the older members of the community; this is less the case in communities like Iskaya, which are more distant. The so-called *residentes* – who are in fact the non-residents since they reside in the city – still own land in the community, and because of their non-rural activities command a degree of economic power and political influence. In Guaqui, another lakeside community, the meetings of the community now tend to take place on Saturdays to enable the *residentes* to be there. In some circumstances, it seems, community meetings even take place in El Alto, since it is more convenient for the *residentes*. In Iskaya, Feliciano López works during the week in El Alto as a shoemaker, while Jhonny Castillo is a bricklayer who returns at weekends to tend his small plot of land. In the south of Oruro, farther from the city, we were told that *residentes* were returning in substantial numbers to take advantage of the boom in quinua production. Antonio Maraza told us how this cut across the cultural practices of the Killaka: the *residentes* were keen to cash in on production for export, whereas 'our custom is to produce only for family consumption'.

The growing salience of *residentes* in the political affairs of the Altiplano appears to have widened the gap between the grass roots in communities and their titular authorities. 'The authorities tend to be interested primarily in political and party matters rather than in issues such as [agricultural] production,' says Eva Colque, director of the Fundación Nuna, which works in four separate Altipl[munities. According to Colque, herself from a community Achacachi, 'relations between the authorities and their ba̲_̲_̲ ̲.̲.̲a̲v̲c̲ become ever more distant'. One of the reasons for this is that their visions of things no longer coincide. Typically, the *residentes* are concerned to use their resources to better their properties and enhance their prestige through public works, whereas the *bases* in rural areas are more interested in improving their crops or building irrigation systems. 'Neither the *sindicato* nor the *ayllu* are very interested in the productive aspects,' says Colque, 'they are more concerned with building up their own political influence in other spheres, often as a stepping stone to political office.'

Living standards in the Altiplano

Statistical studies of living standards in Bolivia consistently show that levels of poverty, however measured, are higher in the rural highlands than in most other parts of the country. They also show significant differences within the highlands, with living standards higher in communities in the Lake Titicaca region in the north than farther south in Oruro and (in particular) in Potosí. In part this is due to the more favourable conditions for crop and dairy production in the Titicaca region, whereas farther south and at higher altitudes communities tend to depend more on the rearing of sheep and llamas, used variously for their meat and their wool, with small plots used to grow potatoes.

Throughout the Altiplano, the scarcity of productive land in relation to the numbers living in the region has meant two things over the years. First, there has been huge outwards migration, to the cities, to the tropics (through colonization) and to other countries, notably to Argentina, but also places farther afield, such as Spain. Secondly, those that remain have to supplement their meagre agricultural income from other activities, such as production of handicrafts, fishing (where appropriate), transport and by commercial activities of various sorts. A central part of family income also comes from work obtained during temporary migration each year. In some places, agriculture is mainly for subsistence while the bulk of people's income comes from other sources. Producers complain regularly that agricultural prices in the cities are kept low, providing little incentive for them to market such traditional fare as potatoes.

The increase in growth in other sectors of the economy since 2003 does not appear to have changed this panorama in any fundamental way. Though municipalities enjoy larger revenue streams as a result of the higher taxes imposed on natural gas companies, much of this money seems to be focused on urban problems (such as building schools or paving streets) rather than rural ones. Of those we interviewed, all complained that agricultural prices remained stagnant and that the increase in demand noted in urban areas had not translated into sustainably higher prices for their products, while they found themselves paying more for products such as rice and sugar produced in the eastern lowlands. Low agricultural prices, we were repeatedly told, are exploited by Peruvians who cross the frontier to buy produce only to sell it at far higher prices in their own country. And, as we have seen, organizations such as *ayllus* and *sindicatos* also come under fire for not standing up for the material interests of those they represent. In Santa Cruz, by contrast, there are strong producer organizations that are able to remonstrate with the government on matters such as prices, credit and preferential markets. According to Roxana Liendo, a former vice-minister for rural development in the Morales administration, the absence of public policy to support small peasant farmers – who voted massively for Evo Morales in 2005 and 2009 – became increasingly evident by 2009 and 2010. 'I don't think the development model has changed,' she says; 'we continue with an agro-industrial model in which Santa Cruz is the axis of food production.'

The clear exception to this rule is quinua, described by Liendo as 'the soya of the Altiplano'. Quinua is a grain for which the market price has rocketed in recent years in response to strong export demand, particularly in European countries and in North America. Previously quinua was a grain that was consumed almost entirely in the domestic market, but its health-giving properties have turned it into a 'must-buy' in the breakfast food market in developed countries. Rising prices on the domestic market mean that only around 20 per cent of production is consumed locally while 80 per cent is now exported. Clearly, this boom has brought benefits to those small farmers on the Altiplano who produce it. Many are no longer so small, and enterprising businessmen, some from Santa Cruz, have also cashed in, providing tools, capital and inputs. The area sown with quinua has increased dramatically, particularly in Oruro, which is now the main area of production. In the case of Killaka communities, with a population of around 50,000, more than half now produce quinua.

Like many boom commodities, however, quinua has brought as many problems as it has solved. It has greatly increased inequalities in the areas where it is produced, undermining community cohesion. Because prices are so high, it exacerbates the problem of the *residentes*, who are only too keen to use their land for such a profitable crop, but who, in Rudy Huayllas's words, 'end up living in luxury homes in Oruro, driving the latest in fast cars'. It has become the main source of conflict over landholding in this area, and a serious aggravating factor to long-standing divisions between Potosí and Oruro. There are also serious ecological costs. Agronomists agree that mono-cultivation of quinua quickly exhausts the relatively poor soils of the Altiplano. In the past, the land was fertilized by the dung from llama herds, but today there is less animal husbandry and more quinua production, so this is no longer the case. Instead, farmers resort to chemicals. Quinua production has led to the abandonment of crop rotation. The poor soils of the Altiplano also require land to lie fallow for extensive periods after crops are harvested, and this is no longer happening. Traditional forms of land management, such as the *bofedales* (humid pastures), are also falling into disuse because of quinua production.

Peasant incomes have also benefited in recent years from the Morales government's policy of extending subsidies (or *bonos*) to specific sectors of the population. Those we interviewed were enthusiastic about these, claiming that they made a significant difference to family incomes. In the case of Renta Dignidad, for example, two old-age pensioners over sixty could expect a monthly income of 400 bolivianos (around US$57), a considerable sum in terms of average family incomes in the Altiplano. The peasant leaders from around Huarina were in no doubt as to the positive effects of the *bonos*. 'Thanks to the nationalization [of hydrocarbons], we have achieved the IDH [Direct Tax on Hydrocarbons] and the three *bonos*, as well as programmes such as Evo Cumple and Mi Agua,' said one. 'Where did the money go before? It went to Santa Cruz and Cochabamba to pay for large-scale public works.' Others are more critical of the use of the *bonos*. According to Roxana Liendo, they do not reach the more remote communities where poverty rates are most acute. 'Nor', she claims, 'do they do anything to help people increase their incomes from production nor indeed reduce inequality.' The problem of access to the system of *bonos* was also highlighted by Joaquín Castillo in Iskaya. He experienced huge bureaucratic difficulties and expense in claiming the Renta Dignidad for his father, whose identity had been appropriated by someone else.

Inclusion

Probably the main benefits from the Morales administration that people pointed to in our interviews were the changes in attitude brought about by the election of the son of indigenous peasants as president of Bolivia. Indeed, despite the criticisms we heard of the shortcomings of government policy, no one we met challenged the notion that Evo's election was a hugely significant event. 'He is one of us; he is part of the family,' says Rudy Huayllas. 'As one of the first Aymaran presidents, as well as an Orureño, we identify with him, many people [here] knew him when he was young.' While the indigenous leaders of south Oruro are critical of some of his government's policies, they remain respectful of his authority. 'Here we do not uproot people,' Rudy claims; 'we give them time to put things right, time to reflect.'

For those organized in both *sindicatos* and in *ayllus*, the passage and final approval of the 2009 constitution brought some fundamental changes to the country. 'This is something which united us all,' says Rudy, 'it was the banner of the indigenous peoples of Bolivia.' But as one of the Killaka *mallkus* noted, 'we still have to put the new constitution into practice, to fully realize our rights'. Similarly, the leaders of the *sindicatos* around Huarina were effusive in their praise for the constitutional changes brought about. As one put it, 'the new constitution, the Plurinational State, the rights of indigenous peoples, the rights of women, they're many significant advances that have been achieved'. Roxana Liendo also underscores the changes that have taken place: 'So far as inclusion is concerned, you cannot deny that there have been improvements and that these are irreversible.' But adopting a rather more critical line, she shares the concern expressed by the *mallku*: 'but when you translate these [rights] into practice in areas like health, education and identity, there are few ways in which to exercise these rights, to make them a reality'. The extent to which indigenous and campesino voices have been brought into patterns of decision-making within the state is still limited.

The rights of women, particularly in the political realm, are an area where there have been major advances in the communities of the Altiplano. Although the Law of Popular Participation of 1996 sets out norms for women's representation in municipal politics, it was by no means assured that these would work in practice. In Aymara culture there is a complementarity between the roles of men and women, but this division of labour has never translated into equality of power; men have always been dominant in public life. But this has been changing, despite the conservatism of Aymaran cultural norms. The new constitution fosters equal eligibility of men and women for all elective positions. While it helps create a framework for behaviour, other factors too have been important in promoting greater equality. In particular, patterns of migration – usually it is men who migrate, leaving women and the elderly in the community – have boosted women's role within the community. Patterns of representation have thus changed, regardless of the law. However, this is not to say that there are no obstacles to gender parity in the political sphere. For example, the election of a woman as a councillor of Ancoraimes, which owed much to pressure from the local *sindicato*, proved something of a breakthrough. However, she was murdered in an attack in El Alto, an egregious example of the sort of harassment women can face in public life. Two other women leaders, elected as local councillors, were slung out of office on trumped-up accusations that they had slept with the mayor and a deputy. A more mundane obstacle to women's empowerment, particularly in more remote communities, is the inability to be fluent in Spanish. In spite of the changes that have taken place within the bureaucracy in Bolivia, it remains hugely difficult to intercede in government matters without a good knowledge of Spanish. And although the state offers some training to those who are elected as councillors, this is provided in Spanish, not in Aymara or Quechua. It is, however, worth drawing attention to the fact that as women take on public responsibilities, they are becoming role models for the next generation.

Conclusions

Though the government and its policies are subject to criticism on the Altiplano, and though some of the more elevated promises made by Evo have yet to be fulfilled, there remains a profound respect for Bolivia's president in this part of the country as 'one of us'. The level of electoral support for Morales in those elections in which he was a candidate between 2005 and 2009 – two presidential elections and a recall referendum (2008) – provide eloquent testimony to this sense of loyalty. Even though opposition may build up at the national level before the 2014 elections, it seems probable that (assuming he stands again) Evo will be able to count on the support of the majority of communities across the Altiplano. And such is the residual strength of community feeling that it is the community which tends to vote en bloc, rather than it being the decision of the individual voter.

However, as we have seen, the Morales administration, despite many valued achievements, has so far failed to come up with the policies required to tackle poverty and inequality in rural communities on a sustainable basis. There is little by way of new thinking, still less practice, on how to increase rural productivity, while the price structure tends to provide little by way of stimulus to highland campesinos. Small-scale producers are still not getting sufficient support from the government, either as credit or as incentives to production. The problem of the land and its subdivision remains a key item on the agenda, just as it was in the 1950s. The various policies introduced since then to tackle this thorny but central issue have largely failed to make much impact. Migration has tended to be the main safety valve, but this has caused major problems elsewhere (as we shall see in the next chapter), not least in the rapid urbanization of El Alto and other cities.

Here popular organization, whether in *sindicatos* or in *ayllus*, has largely failed to tackle the problems affecting the productive potential of the Altiplano. All too often, their leaders have been bought off or sidetracked into other activities that do little to resolve the problems of those who select them. All in all, by 2012 social organization in the Altiplano was at a low ebb. Social movements often come into their own in articulating discontent at times of crisis – such as in the period 2000–03 – but then fail to sustain the pressure when circumstances change. Their inability to coalesce into structured organizations limits their capacity to achieve lasting change. And where that organizational capacity exists, as in many places on the Altiplano, it is easy for the leaders to become absorbed in other activities, including within the state, and thus to become removed from the everyday concerns of those whom they purport to represent.

Finally, there is the concern about a problem in the making. As we have already noted, the potential exists for the development of conflict between indigenous campesinos of different groups. This is particularly the case where issues of the use of natural resources are concerned: possibly mining but also the production of quinua, and eventually conflict over water. Such conflict would be underscored by different visions of how people understand '*vivir bien*'.

3 | EL ALTO: A CITY OF MIGRANTS

Whether you arrive in La Paz by air or by road, El Alto is the point of entry. It is a city of near on a million people, and from the rim of the deep crater in which La Paz is built, it spreads out across the flat Altiplano, a plain broken up by individual houses and communities that separates the eastern and western cordilleras of the Andes. It is a city where a vast number of people live in poverty, a city of migrants from the surrounding rural areas, a young city without the imprint of history or of Hispanic colonial culture. Above all, it is a predominantly Aymara city, distinct in many ways from the next-door city of La Paz, from which it became a distinct administrative and political entity in 1988.

But seen from the angle of La Paz, El Alto is also the point at which the city connects with the rest of the country. It is the point through which much of its food and commerce arrives; it is also the point through which most of its energy requirements are channelled. As such El Alto occupies a strategic position. Its main arteries radiate fan-like from La Ceja, literally 'The Brow', where the twisting roads up the hillsides from the centre of La Paz meet the Altiplano. To the west, the Avenida Juan Pablo II stretches in a straight line out towards Lake Titicaca and the Peruvian frontier posts at Desaguadero and Copacabana. To the south-east, the Avenida 6 de Marzo points in the direction of Oruro, from there connecting to Bolivia's other main cities, Cochabamba, Santa Cruz, Potosí and Sucre. In between, a third artery leads to the nearby town of Viacha and (eventually) to the frontier with Chile.

In between and along these three prongs, a maze of settlements have grown up over the years. Much of the construction is simple; buildings of concrete and red breeze blocks with corrugated-iron roofs are the main architectural idiom, constructed along chessboard grid matrices. The town has an unfinished look, as building stops when the money runs out. Yet the pattern of economic accumulation is unmistakeable, with buildings nearer to the central commercial districts now reaching for the sky, five, six or seven storeys high. A new, esoteric and flamboyant architectural style has emerged, quintessentially *alteño* in character, with buildings painted in bright hues, adorned with baroque stucco twirls and with a predilection for coloured polarized-glass façades. Several have built small chalets on the roofs, from which the owners overlook their immediate neighbourhood.

Administratively, El Alto is divided into fourteen districts. Though the boundaries between these communities are by no means clear to the outside eye, each has its particular characteristics – its urban centre, its central plaza, its communal and church buildings. Each also tends to be peopled predominantly from particular sectors of the workforce or different places of origin. While the northern districts are largely Aymaran, mainly people from rural areas, those of the south are more mixed. But despite this community fragmentation, an *alteño* identity has been forged and a pride in being autonomous of La Paz, the city from which it first emerged as an overflow suburb some fifty years ago.

The history of El Alto goes back to when the first pockets of settlement took root in the 1940s and 1950s. Until then El Alto was basically a railway station with its sidings and warehouses, at the point at which the steeply inclined railway up from the centre of La Paz finally reached the edge of the Altiplano. Like the road links of today, the railway split into three at La Ceja, one leading to Oruro and the south, another to the port of Guaqui on Lake Titicaca (and with a steamer link from there to Puno in Peru), and a third leading to Arica, on the Chilean coast. When the airport at El Alto was constructed in the 1950s, it was still in open country. The process of urbanization began in earnest in the mid-1960s, particularly during the government of General René Barrientos.

Initially, El Alto was just an overflow area for La Paz. As the city of La Paz grew rapidly in population in these years, the land available for housing for new generations became increasingly scarce, with communities perched precariously on ever-steeper inclines along the sides of the crater in which the city nestles. In El Alto, where the land surface is flat and physical barriers to urban growth are absent, there were no such constraints.

As it grew rapidly in size, El Alto became a pole of attraction for migrants from all over the Altiplano and, indeed, farther afield. Besides the overflow and new generations from La Paz, there were housing projects for factory workers, journalists, miners and public sector workers. Peasants from the Altiplano continued to arrive, both to secure their future and educate their children, often maintaining a double residence both in their communities and in El Alto. In the 1980s, Quechua miners who lost their jobs owing to structural adjustment settled both in the north and south of the city. In the 1980s and 1990s, El Alto became one of Latin America's fastest-growing cities, with an annual population growth rate of 9–10 per cent. Since then demographic growth has slowed to between 5 and 6 per cent, but El Alto continues to attract new settlers who build their homes ever farther from the main urban hubs of La Ceja, Villa Dolores and Ciudad Satélite. Once out in the sticks, the airport is now located squarely in the middle of this sprawling conurbation. The exact size of the population is difficult to quantify, but when the results of the 2012 census become known, it is almost certain that the population of El Alto – which surpassed that of La Paz some years back – will top a million. One in ten Bolivians will be an *alteño*. And more and more, as the town comes of age, the major part of its population will be young and will be born here.

When people first settled in El Alto, their experience was one of suffering. The survival of its original citizens was down to their strong sense of communal organization and their refusal to be browbeaten. Norma Soliz first moved to Santiago II, a township close to the road to Oruro, in 1976. She recalls how her barrio at the time was no more than four blocks of houses; the rest was just scrub (*paja brava*) where the animals would roam. 'We managed to get access to water,' she says, 'but the whole community – from grandparents down to small children – depended on a single tap.' Norma, who was the wife of prominent mineworker's leader Justo Pérez, originally came to El Alto from the Siete Suyos mining community in southern Potosí. Her husband had been deported to Argentina during the repression years of the 1960s, and Norma eventually settled in Santiago II along with other mineworkers and their families, when she managed to get a job in the headquarters of Comibol in La Paz. 'From the outset

we were organized,' she says; 'we had a neighbou[r]
[*junta vecinal*], we had a *sindicato*, and a housewive[s]
    Another early settler was Antonia Rodríguez. She
Primero de Mayo, close to the road to Viacha, in 1982.
Potosí, she had lived previously in a cramped area just   ...os
Aires Avenue in central La Paz. She recalls that 'when we first arrived
here [in Primero de Mayo] it was just pampa, with stones and a few
sheep. There was no water or electricity. We had to bring water all
the way from La Ceja to fill the tank. We washed our clothes in the
river. It was hard.' She also remembers how the advances made at
the time were the result of local initiative. 'Among the first things
we did was to organize a *junta de vecinos*. We organized a blockade
[*bloqueo*] of the airport to get electricity in 1983 and 1984. We organized another *bloqueo* to get water,' she says. 'It always took force to
achieve anything.' Her community then managed to construct the
main plaza, hitherto just mounds of rubble, and then, with some
help from the local church, to construct the neighbourhood school.
But, she recalls, 'we spent a lot of time in meetings'.
    Isabel Atencio, a leader of the Urbanización 18 de Mayo area, also
on the road to Oruro, was a manufacturing worker from La Paz: she
tells of the hardship they suffered at first, when they lost their jobs
as a consequence of the structural adjustment policies pursued in
the mid-1980s, and how they had to organize to get anything done.
The experience brought many women out of the home and into
local politics.
    The strength of El Alto as a community has much to do with
its spirit of organization. On the one hand this is a legacy of the
communitarian traditions of Andean rural communities from which
most *alteños* originally hail. Then there is the trade union experience
brought by miners who settled locally in the 1980s. Finally, it is a
result of the tasks facing newly established communities in gaining
access to basic services, such as water, electricity and education.
Particularly in the early days, it was group solidarity which led to
the supply of basic urban services. The most important institution
in this sense was the *junta vecinal*, the neighbourhood committee in
which most *alteños* at one point or another have become involved.
Altogether, there are an estimated seven hundred *juntas vecinales* in El

Alto. Their number constantly increases as new communities emerge on the periphery of the urban areas, accommodating new waves of migrants to the city. The *juntas vecinales* are grouped together according to the districts to which they belong, the fourteen districts into which the city is divided. These districts, in turn, elect the Federación de Juntas Vecinales, the Fejuve. The Fejuve has become the prime actor in representing the interests of *alteños*, more so – it would seem – than the elected mayor and councillors.

However, there are many other types of organization in which people participate and which also have a voice in the politics of the district. There are, for instance, the parents' associations, which are organized in every school in El Alto. These are mainly concerned with educational issues, but often this concern merges into other areas, such as the price of clothing or the tariffs charged by taxi drivers and bus companies. They are also concerned with problems of insecurity in their neighbourhoods. There are a myriad of church organizations, reflecting the parochial structure of El Alto, but combining not just Catholic organizations but also fast-expanding Evangelical churches. Then there are professional organizations and trade unions representing different groups within the workforce. They vary widely in type and activity, but one of the most numerous is the *gremialistas*, the street traders who work the city's many markets. In practice, the citizens of El Alto are likely to be involved in more than one type of organization, seeking to make their own particular combination of interests heard at the wider level. As one seasoned observer has put it, El Alto is 'hyper-organized'.

For many in El Alto, it was the events of October 2003 which stand out as a landmark of popular organization. It was the so-called 'gas war' which led to the ouster of President Gonzalo Sánchez de Lozada and the initiation of a new period in Bolivian politics. It was in the streets of El Alto that the resistance to the government and its policies took shape. The campaign against policies to sell Bolivian gas to the United States through a pipeline to Chile became a catalyst for a range of demands and complaints, linking local issues to much broader ones at the national and even international levels. According to Alfredo Cahuaya, a community leader in El Alto for the last twenty-five years, 'the discussion over natural resources unleashed connections with other levels of analysis'. He claims that 'October 2003 was significant in helping to create an identity as *alteños*' and that it 'greatly helped raise the self-esteem of *alteños*'. But, as well as a victory, October 2003 stands out in the collective memory as a moment of loss, with sixty-seven of their number being mown down by army troops, and many others wounded. The repatriation of Sánchez de Lozada and some of his ministers from the United States to stand trial for these killings remains a key demand and a source of deep rancour for many in El Alto.

In retrospect, the events of October 2003 and their immediate antecedents stand as a symbol of what can be achieved when people work together around a single objective that forges unity among an otherwise disparate population. With leadership from the Fejuve, an institution that came into its own as a political actor in 2003, the 'gas war' brought together new leaderships and new communities of interest. According to Carlos Revilla, who leads the Urban Programme at the umbrella NGO UNITAS, 'interests were linked in such a way as to flow upwards from grass roots to their representatives and downwards from the leadership to the grass roots'. The October protests also illustrated the importance of communications – the media and mobile phones – in the process of mobilization, as well as highlighting the strategic importance of El Alto as a city: it was the threat of energy and food being cut off to La Paz which forced Sánchez de Lozada to send in the troops, specifically to restore blocked supplies of gasoline and diesel from the Senkata depot out on the road towards Oruro. It was the demands that emerged from the 'gas war' which were to provide the policy framework for the next five or six years, the so-called 'October Agenda'. The strength and resistance of *alteños* was strongly linked to levels of participation in the Fejuve, a democratic space where all would stand by the decision of the majority.

Still, there remains considerable debate as to the significance of these events, a debate that has influenced discussion of how *alteño* politics has evolved since then, especially since the election of Evo Morales in 2005. To what extent was this just an outgrowth of the previous history of local organization and a spirit of resistance? Or was it an expression or the flourishing of an indigenous, Aymaran identity in the midst of a neocolonial state?

Popular power and participation

In the manner in which they developed, the *juntas vecinales* were highly participative institutions. Broadly, they served the interests and demands of those who composed them, particularly relating to the provision of basic services. At the same time, there was always the counter-tendency for them to be controlled from above, particularly by political parties and those in government. In the early days, the *consejos de vecinos* were closely connected to the MNR. The advent of democratic politics in the early 1980s and the increasing electoral weight of El Alto at the time meant that political parties sought to win influence among the *juntas vecinales*. The relationship between the central government and the local administration on the one hand and the neighbourhood-based social movements on the other was always one of tension between top-down politics and the bottom-up pressures exerted by grassroots movements. In the 1980s and 1990s, the most influential political parties in El Alto were Conciencia de Patria (Condepa), a populist movement which gained considerable traction in the city as well as in La Paz, and the Movimiento de Izquierda Revolucionario (MIR), a centre-left grouping whose leader, Jaime Paz, became president in 1989. Both parties were noted for using public works (*obras*) as a way of building political support. Such projects often responded to deeply felt specific needs in the community, and community leaders often went along with them. Antonia Rodríguez recalls, for instance, how people in her barrio responded well to the activities of young *miristas* who offered to help with community projects.

In 1996, the Sánchez de Lozada government (1993–97) introduced its programme of administrative decentralization, known as Participación Popular. This increased the roles and responsibilities of municipal governments, creating at the same time a system of public oversight, the *comités de vigilancia*. Among other things, Participación Popular had the effect of dividing up the communities on a territorial basis, weakening the spirit of class consciousness that had pervaded El Alto. According to Norma Soliz, people at the time were reluctant to become involved in Participación Popular, but at the same time they saw some of the economic advantages it could bring. Class consciousness was also diluted by the economic reforms of the 1980s and 1990s, which encouraged the growth of commercial activities in El Alto at the expense of productive ones. The growth of the 'informal sector' helped transform working relations, undermine community solidarity, and encourage an increasingly competitive ethos in the labour market. In this context, the *juntas vecinales* tended to become key mediators between the state and society and, increasingly, a clientelistic nexus by which those in authority sought to influence local politics through programmes of *obras*.

The events of 2003, which began as a neighbourhood protest against the introduction of new municipal taxes and terminated with the expulsion of Sánchez de Lozada as president, represented an important shift in local politics, with an explosion of upwards pressure on local elites and, finally, on the central government itself. The protests that surrounded the 'gas war' involved intense mobilization by local groups across El Alto and the displacement of many of those who had previously run the Fejuve in El Alto. In the words of Fany Nina, who went on to become the first ever woman president of the Fejuve, '2003 was when we acquired consciousness of social justice'.

The 'gas war' effectively challenged many of the presuppositions about the way in which local politics worked, creating important new spaces for public participation. It engendered a new sense of unity in what had become previously a fragmented scene in which, according to Alfredo Cahuaya, 'petty jealousies' had made working with neighbourhood groups highly problematic. The gas issue created animated discussion across the city in ways that questioned the neoliberal policies of the Sánchez de Lozada government. Again, according to Cahuaya, it raised questions about 'why, if we possess such abundant natural resources, are we so poor'. In the opinion of Isabel Atencio, however, it was the killing of the sixty-seven *alteños* which really galvanized the whole community, producing an unprecedented unity of spirit. 'The conflict arose from the anger of the people, but rather than a "gas war" as such, it was the massacre of an unarmed people.'

The election of the MAS government in December 2005 equally created a widespread sense of excitement in El Alto. Evo Morales won by a much higher proportion than in most other parts of the country. In the years that followed, the city became a bastion of support for the party, with the involvement of some social movements in the design and execution of public policy. However, Evo's popularity at the national level did not necessarily translate into the popularity of MAS candidates at the local level. The issue of water became a key item of policy, reflecting the experience of Cochabamba a few years previously. Debate centred on the role of Aguas de Illimani, a privatized water provider and subsidiary of the French multinational Suez. Aguas de Illimani was eventually taken back into national ownership following a protracted dispute between the government and the company over its investment record in El Alto. Particularly those neighbourhoods on the periphery of the city, generally those with the lowest incomes and the greatest need for water provision, complained at both the failure of the company to provide proper arrangements for water supply and the high costs of getting connected. These were the areas where the returns on capital invested were likely to be lowest. In 2006, Evo Morales appointed Abel Mamani, the president of the Fejuve in 2004 and 2005 when there were major mobilizations over the water issue, as his minister responsible for water and the environment. This is seen by some, such as Carlos Revilla, as a point of inflection, the moment at which social movement leaders began to be co-opted and the links between the grass roots and leadership in them broke down. Under the new system, both the Fejuve and the Central Obrera Regional (COR), the regional labour confederation, became part of the management of the new state-run water firm, EPSAS.

The story of social movement organization since 2006 has tended to be one of increasing atomization. On the one hand, with the issue of Aguas de Illimani resolved, there were few 'big issues' to unite this disparate and heterogeneous community. Several of our interviewees pointed to the fragmentation of demands, into purely local issues such as drainage and the adornment of plazas. On the other hand, as they also observed, there was a process by which some grassroots leaders after 2006 became absorbed into the state, whether within the municipality or within the apparatus of central government. The old practice of *'peguismo'* – jobs for supporters – which had been criticized so vehemently during the period of neoliberal government, appeared to re-emerge in new forms. According to Cahuaya, whose activities in community organization are concentrated in District 4 on the road out to the lake, whereas leaders in 2003 found themselves obliged to listen to the grass roots for fear that these would overwhelm them, 'now it is very different; there is a divorce at this level'. He claims that ties of clientelism are reinforced by traditional practices of *compadrazgo*.[1] His view is to some extent echoed by that of Freddy Quilo, who works primarily with youth groups in a parish in Rio Seco. He claims that 'the problem lies in when they [the *juntas vecinales*] become politicized and begin to respond more to a party and self-interest than to the interest of their barrios and their grass roots'.

According to Isabel Atencio in Urbanización 18 de Mayo, as the *juntas vecinales* have become more politicized, the space available for discussion and public participation has diminished. Her opinion was echoed by Mercedes Condori from District 4, a former leader of the Fejuve, who said that 'before there was consultation between the different levels, and decisions were taken from below through the use of regular meetings of district presidents'. She claimed that this had fallen largely into disuse in recent years, resulting in a 'deterioration of the Fejuve'. This breakdown in levels of discussion and participation has led people to seek other outlets for protest, such as the Federation of School Parents (the Federación de Padres de Familia). This conducted a series of demonstrations in March 2012, albeit around local and specific, rather than more general, issues.

We encountered widespread criticism of the MAS mayor of El Alto, Edgar Patana, and the failure of local leaderships to take issue with him. In theory, under the law of Participación Popular, it is up to the *juntas vecinales*, and in particular the Fejuve, to elect the members of the *comité de vigilancia*, responsible for oversight or social control of municipal activities. In practice, however, exercising this oversight is not so straightforward. It is the mayor at the district level, the *sub-alcalde*, who takes administrative decisions at the local level. In most cases in El Alto, the *sub-alcalde* is appointed by the mayor, although there have been some occasions when the *sub-alcalde* has been chosen by popular vote. The *comité de vigilancia* therefore is

---

1 Literally the relationship between a child's parents and godparents; in this context, political sponsorship.

selected by the *juntas vecinales* to exercise social control, but the mayor (or *sub-alcalde*) tends to run controls on their remit.

Moreover, there are limitations on who becomes a leader at the local level. Participation is limited to property owners within the neighbourhood and therefore excludes many other people. This reduces the range of issues taken up to, mainly, those of urban infrastructure. Freddy Quilo points to the fact that young people – who make up the majority of the population in El Alto (the average age of the population is twenty-four) – are poorly represented. They often find it hard to become involved in the *juntas vecinales* and other types of neighbourhood organization, made up of older people, over the age of thirty. The process of consultation and oversight therefore suffers from some serious limitations in the way the system works on an everyday basis.

The ambiguous nature of the structure of power in local *alteño* politics is highlighted by the experience of Fany Nina. Elected as an outsider in 2010 on a wave of sympathy for more open and effective leadership in the Fejuve, she soon ran into difficulties with the established (male) interest groups represented in this body, particularly among the executive committee of the Fejuve. She recounts how her efforts to push ahead with much-needed projects, particularly in the health sector, and others that had been relegated for various reasons, met with dogged resistance from the executive leaders. Nina herself told us how there were various attempts to remove her, culminating in a traffic 'accident' in which she was badly hurt and was thereafter replaced as president. According to Mercedes Condori, Nina was chucked out because 'she said what she thought' and she was a victim of 'the selfish attitude of the men'. It may well have been related to the former argument since Nina was critical of the implementation of the October Agenda by the MAS. Harassment of women involved in politics has been such as to require the approval in 2012 of a law penalizing such actions, however difficult they may be to prove.

At the centre of this awkward relationship is the way in which public works are carried out, whether by *sub-alcaldes*, the municipality of El Alto, the central government or the presidential 'Evo Cumple' programme. Often bereft of public services, people in El Alto value the programmes of *obras* provided by the authorities, whether simply parochial or more ambitious (such as providing hospitals and schools). Yet, in recent years, the ability of local people to become involved in the planning and execution of public works – so much a feature of El Alto in the early years – has become seriously circumscribed. *Obras* become a way in which established leaders can legitimize themselves politically and curry political support, especially at times of elections. As Mercedes Condori remarked, 'local leaders have status because they have achieved *obras*; I maintained mine for this reason'. So rather than forming part of a planned development programme, these *obras* are often seen as ends in themselves.

The decline in the status of the Fejuve as a channel for public participation has led to the increased salience of other types of organization. As we have seen, the Parents' Federation has recently emerged as a more vociferous organization, but one concerned more with educational issues than other forms of public provision. But it too suffers from divisions within its ranks, a split between the largely Aymaran northern districts and the more mixed ones of the south. Other types of organization are today far less active than ten years ago. The NGOs that once provided sustenance to popular movements face major problems of funding and have reduced their activities notably. The churches too take a less activist role than previously, concerned more with their own particular concerns at the parish level rather than taking up more global issues. The one type of organization that has gained enormous power and influence in recent decades is the *gremiales*. The *gremiales* represent the thousands of street traders who have greatly multiplied in number over the last twenty-five years. However, they seldom articulate community interests as a whole, as opposed to their own narrower self-interest as traders.

Living standards, employment and the economy

Whatever you may need to acquire, you are likely to find it in the 16 de Julio market, which takes place twice a week, on Thursdays and Sundays. What's on offer ranges from nails up to the latest in four-by-fours, costing tens of thousands of dollars. People come to the market from all over El Alto as well as from La Paz and farther afield. A constant stream of people wind their way up the steep slopes from

La Paz towards El Alto in search of cheap deals. Spreading out from the Plaza 16 de Julio, the market takes over the whole barrio, blue and orange awnings stretching as far as the eye can see down seemingly identical streets. This is the freest of free markets, most of the produce imported as contraband, much of it originating in China and Korea. There's not a whiff of tariffs or import controls here. The scale of the market is, in a sense, a monument to free trade.

The 16 de Julio market is a symbol of the primacy of commerce in today's El Alto. Some 70 per cent of economic activity in the city is thought to be dedicated to commerce. It is for this reason that the *gremialistas*, and behind them much wealthier commercial interests, have become such a dominant force in the city. Aymara people, of course, are well known for their commercial acumen, and this is as true among Aymarans across the lake in Peru as it is in Bolivia. However, the expansion of the commercial sector in El Alto owes much to the economic transformation that has taken place since the mid-1980s when Bolivia's experiment in economic liberalization began. The freeing of markets led to a transformation in the labour market in El Alto. Carlos Revilla has estimated that manufacturing employed nearly 40 per cent of the labour force in the 1980s, whereas this proportion was down to 23 per cent in 2001, and has probably fallen further since. By contrast, he shows how the informal sector has grown at a vertiginous rate. Those who have lost their jobs in manufacturing have been joined by the influx of migrants from rural areas, and specific groups of workers who lost their jobs owing to structural adjustment in the 1980s. Many of the estimated 27,000 mineworkers who were made redundant – 'relocalized', to use the euphemism of the time – lost their homes in the mining encampments and eventually came to settle in El Alto. Their number included Justo Pérez and Norma Soliz.

As well as a protest against gas exports through Chile, October 2003 was also a protest against social injustice in El Alto, and the prevalence of poverty there. The October Agenda included the scrapping of Decree 21060, the law passed in 1985 that created the basis for economic liberalization, introduced at a time of chaotic hyperinflation. By voting for Evo Morales as president in December 2005, the people of El Alto were voting for a new deal in the economic sphere. It was hoped that this would lead to more prosperous times for *alteños* and the expansion of stable employment for its inhabitants with all the social benefits that this might imply. The extent to which these hopes have been realized is mixed.

There is no doubt that several years of economic growth in Bolivia have had a positive impact on El Alto. The construction boom that has taken place there is in evidence in all parts of the city, as one- and two-storey buildings have given way to multi-story edifices and even (in some places) tower blocks. More modestly, many householders have built on an extra room or a second floor. The demand for construction workers has pushed up wages in this sector, sometimes dramatically. Whereas a bricklayer in 2005 would typically earn 50 bolivianos a day (around US$7), the going rate in 2012 was around 200 bolivianos. Skilled labourers were particularly in demand. Unemployment levels are difficult to measure in a place like El Alto, but according to some estimates these reached 16 per cent in the years of economic difficulty in the late 1990s, compared with 10 per cent then nationally. Increases in the minimum wage, decreed annually by the government, have only a limited impact in places like El Alto, given the extent to which most people work in an unregulated and informal job market where remuneration pays no heed to official minimums. Income per head of the population has certainly increased – as in other parts of Bolivia – but it remains difficult to say by how much. Anecdotal information suggests that the hard times of the 1990s are over, and families now enjoy considerably more disposable income. According to Isabel Atencio, 'People now have more money, and use it for construction. Then, the neighbourhood fiesta had fizzled out because there was no money around. This has changed in the last five years, and people dance at all times of the year. People buy rice in *quintales*. Small corner shops have turned into [larger] stores.'

The introduction of systems of allowances for specific vulnerable groups in the population appears to have had considerable impact, not just within these narrow sectors but to the benefit of families as a whole. Again, in the words of Isabel Atencio, the introduction of insurance cover for pregnant women 'is a great thing'. For someone who has no medical insurance, the proposal to create a universal health service 'is very necessary'. Likewise, the Renta Dignidad, the monthly payment to those over sixty, has provided some protection to the elderly. 'I think this is a very positive step,' says Freddy Quilo in District 4. In Santiago II, where there are a large number of pensioners, Norma Soliz says that 'the *bonos* have helped a great deal'. The Bono Juancito Pinto, a payment to children of primary school age, has been a 'source of joy', in the words of Antonia Rodríguez, though she doubts whether the Bono Juana Azurduy (paid to nursing mothers) has had the same impact. According to others, such as Quilo, little of the Juancito Pinto gets spent on educational materials; rather it is used by parents to provide presents for their children which otherwise they would be ill able to afford. It also gets spent by the kids themselves on sweets and crisps, he claims.

It is evident, though, that increases in living standards overall have not been shared equally in El Alto, and that there is a growing gap between rich and poor. While there is widespread poverty in most districts, there are clear indications of accumulation of wealth, particularly in the more 'middle-class' neighbourhoods of La Ceja and Ciudad Satélite. Even in Santiago II, where poverty is widespread, there are clear indications of new-found wealth. Norma Soliz points to the large houses being constructed along the principal avenues and around the main square. She has no doubt that some of this wealth is accumulated from illegal activities, particularly contraband and drug trafficking. 'Often,' she says, 'these businesses carry on behind legal façades, like outfits selling sports clothing.' 'No one', she says, 'wants to name names, to put the bell on the cat.' The existence of an *alteño* bourgeoisie has been a consequence of liberalization, claims Javier Gómez from the CEDLA think tank, a specialist on labour matters. 'Within the commercial sector, management of markets has led to a huge accumulation of power. You can see this clearly in Eloy Salmón [in the heart of La Paz's market district] and in La Ceja, where you will find some of the most expensive real estate in Bolivia.' However, the lifestyles of the wealthy in El Alto differ a great deal from those of economic elites elsewhere in La Paz, particularly in the affluent Zona Sur. Patterns of consumption are very different, and do not take their cue from US styles. Instead of holidays in Miami or the Caribbean, large sums typically are spent on fiestas, carnival and parades such as the Gran Poder. According to Juan Carlos Núñez of Fundación

Jubileo, a Catholic NGO, 'wealthy people [in El Alto] have no wor-
ries about selling *refrescos* on the street while commanding a huge
fortune of their own ... Their houses are a far cry from the chalets of
the Zona Sur with a distinctive architecture of their own.' Often such
buildings constitute a depository below, with space for a truck, with
offices and rented accommodation on intermediate floors, and the
idealized campesino ranch-type structure on the roof, where they live.

However, this is an elite that lives off commerce – legal and
illegal – not production. While there remains a good deal of small-
scale productive enterprise – much of it informal – in El Alto, this
is constantly squeezed by competition from imported goods from
abroad. There are some larger factories, but they tend not to employ
many workers. Victor Pacosillo, an Aymaran entrepreneur who owns
a factory processing quinua for export and making machinery for
quinua producers, argues that what is important is to focus on the
introduction of technology to boost efficiency and productivity, not
to provide employment, though he concedes that this does little to
resolve the problems of un- and underemployment that surround
him in Rio Seco. In the view of Godofredo Sandoval, who has written extensively on El Alto, it is impractical to think of a successful
industrial policy in a place like El Alto. 'No one can compete with
transnational companies and what comes from China,' he says. This
creates a dilemma for those in government, since one of the main
demands of people in El Alto is for stable, secure employment.
When asked what '*vivir bien*' means to them, most people respond
to this effect, rather than referring to community harmony or living
in contact with nature. And although the Morales administration has
taken steps to clamp down on contraband, it seems implausible that
this will have much sustained effect in a country with multiple land
frontiers, which it has great difficulty in controlling.

Towards a more inclusive society?

The issue of ethnic discrimination has been one of the constants in
Bolivian history since earliest colonial times. With the election of Evo
Morales and the inclusion of social movements within the compass
of political decision-making, the MAS government has sought to
reduce exclusion of people on ethnic grounds. It is perhaps premature

to judge the extent to which this has been true in El Alto. As we have suggested above, El Alto is not a uniform city in terms of its ethnic make-up, but is predominantly an Aymaran city. The issue of ethnic unity is an important ingredient, and it is because of his ethnic, as well as his social, origins that Evo maintains a high degree of legitimacy in the city of migrants. This is not just a symbolic issue, but represents a distinct change in the way in which *alteños* feel about themselves and towards the outside world. When asked what she thought was the most significant change to come about since 2003, Maria Luisa Urrelo – who works as a community leader in District 4 and has close contacts with the Catholic Church there – answered:

> It has been the ending of overt discrimination. No longer are *indios* and *cholos* reviled in the way they were. The *señora de pollera*[2] used to be treated very badly. All this has changed with Evo. Discrimination still exists, but it is not nearly so overt. Racism can take place the other way [i.e. towards '*blancos*'] but there has been a huge advance towards mutual respect in society. Before you could not get a job in a hotel if you wore a *pollera*. That's no longer true.

Adding to this, Freddy Quilo commented that 'there is now pride in being indigenous. There's no need to be submissive. This is one of the biggest changes.'

The status of women in society also seems to have undergone a big change in El Alto, even though it is a society which continues to be dominated by men. In part, the changing attitudes towards women are a recognition of the role played by women in the genesis of El Alto. This came out clearly in our interview with Norma Soliz, who stressed how women took over as heads of household in her barrio in the 1980s, as their husbands left for places like Santa Cruz in search of work. Women took a central role in the affairs of the locality and in the *junta vecinal*: 'The mothers' clubs helped provide food, security and health. We promoted handicrafts among the women. We built centres for distribution of milk in four districts [...] We became a powerful organization, with some 450

---

2 A woman wearing the ample skirts that typify indigenous women in Bolivia.

women involved. These were the people that organized Santiago II.' While acknowledging help from outside agencies, such as the NGO Gregoria Apaza, Soliz was in no doubt as to the historic role played by women in her neighbourhood.

The role played by women in the events of 2003 further increased the legitimacy of women's action, although it certainly did not end feelings of machismo among men. Cleo Quispe, who currently lives in nearby Achocalla but who has worked in El Alto, also underlines how attitudes have changed in recent times. 'One of the main achievements of this government [Evo's] has been to create more equal conditions for men and women. Before, when I lived in the campo, men accorded us little importance. When I first came to the city, most women changed their style of dress. We also changed the language we used.' That's all changed. Women wear their traditional clothes and the use of Aymara in public life is now common. Men have come to respect women's contributions more. When we spoke to Cleo she was dressed elegantly in traditional dress, which is what she wears to work in the Ministry of Production. Several of the women we interviewed had risen to significant political positions, with one – Antonia Rodríguez – becoming a government minister.

Notwithstanding these achievements, there remain significant barriers to social ascent in El Alto, just as in other parts of Bolivia. Perhaps most important are the limitations affecting the educational system. Several of our interviewees commented on the improvements that had taken place in the schools in their neighbourhood, both in terms of infrastructure and in the quality of education imparted to children. Freddy Quilo, who works with young people in particular, claimed that school facilities had improved significantly in his barrio, and that young people are no longer hidebound by the classroom but learn from a wide range of other stimuli, not least the Internet. The problem, he argued, was not so much the schooling children received, but the limitations of the labour market. There were simply no jobs for school leavers. 'Why study sociology, if you can make more money as a *comerciante*?' he asked. The same message came from Hipólito Quispe, a mature student at the Popular University of El Alto (UPEA), who questioned the outlook of the teaching profession. 'They're more interested in their own situation than in education,' he says.

A self-identified Aymaran through and through ('*un aymara neto*'), he also questioned the relevance of bilingual education, a policy espoused by the Morales administration, claiming that Aymara is not the language of economic opportunity. For Verónica Segarrundo, a law student at the UPEA, a new university, the prospects of achieving her ambition to work in the courts were at risk since the UPEA was not considered a 'premier' education institution compared with other, more prestigious universities in La Paz. She complained about the way in which the media portrayed the UPEA as an institution where students did nothing but get drunk.

Finally, the future of El Alto is bedevilled by social problems that affect most large townships in Latin America: crime, social violence, drug trafficking, gang warfare and the like. On these issues, most of those we talked to felt a strong degree of concern and overt criticism for the lack of action on these fronts by the authorities. Indeed, when we conducted these interviews, the murder of two well-known local journalists was galvanizing public opinion, leading to demands that the death penalty be introduced and that neighbourhood vigilantes be allowed to patrol the streets, especially at night. Some areas, like La Ceja, were widely considered no-go zones by many after nightfall. The presence of the police in El Alto was clearly wholly inadequate for dealing with the sort of problems to which they were required to respond. Norma Soliz, for instance, commented that in her neighbourhood there were but four policemen for a barrio with 5,000 homes. She commented that 'they are wholly outnumbered when they have to confront gangs of twenty people or more'. For her, the answer lay in neighbourhood organization, street by street. 'This is citizen security from below,' she claimed, 'and it is giving us positive results.' For Isabel Atencio, too, the answer lies in better community organization and the use of whistles and mobile phones to transmit information quickly; the problem is that people are afraid of reprisals. The penetration of drug culture into the operations of gangs in El Alto is probably far less developed than in other parts of Latin America, but Freddy Quilo attested to the fact that drug consumption in schools was on the increase while 'nobody blows the whistle'. For him, the bigger danger was the omnipresence of alcohol and the fact that drinking starts among pre-adolescents.

Conclusions

The conclusion to be drawn from all this is that the ability of the authorities to respond to the needs and demands of citizens in El Alto is severely limited by the scale of the problems faced and a lack of resources with which to deal with them. Some point to the limited benefits they have received from the nationalization of gas (for which they fought in 2003), whereas people in Tarija (where the gas comes from) have received handsome rewards. The lack of proper employment and the ubiquitous nature of informality create a social milieu with huge problems. The lack of channels of adequate representation and the personal appetites of local politicians, whose main interest often lies in personal advantage and promotion rather than representing the interests of those they supposedly serve, have made the problems worse. In this chapter we have looked at some of the reasons why the Fejuve, for example, has lost the prominence it had previously: the fact that people have put their faith in the government to respond to the problems they face; that some of its leaders have taken on roles in local and national government; and that some of the links between leaders and the grass roots have withered. The atomization of social organization has made local action difficult to orchestrate. The gap between grassroots social movements and the leadership of neighbourhood organizations appears to have grown since 2006. For its part, the state (at different levels) has tended to focus its attention on public works rather than projects that help develop the city's productive potential and thus create much-needed jobs. Where local government in particular fails to respond to longer-term needs, by concentrating on *obras* (which have a short-term political logic) rather than focusing on longer-term needs (such as employment), it is storing up problems for the future.

Still, our interviewees attested that by no means all is negative and that considerable advances have been made in recent years in terms of people's self-esteem and their ability to use their limited organizational resources to deal with seemingly overwhelming problems. Social infrastructure – hospitals, schools and the like – have improved substantially in recent years, as have many people's incomes and their capacity to buy basic goods and services. And perhaps most importantly, and despite growing levels of social inequality and the existence of obstacles to social mobility, there is a strong spirit of self-esteem and one of social inclusion with the erosion of systems of racial and gender discrimination. And perhaps most importantly, the basis for social organization is very much alive; when people feel the need to come out on the street to protest, they are by no means reticent about doing so, as was seen during the *gasolinazo*. The history of El Alto continues to play a significant role in how people view collective action. Understanding this background is important. The role played by social movements in 2003 responded to a growing process of organization over the years and the ways in which neighbourhood action was forged, although the events of that year were triggered partly by conjunctural factors. As we have observed, El Alto is a highly organized place, and the fact that levels of social mobilization vary from location to location and time to time does not alter this in the longer term. Although by no means homogenous in terms of its social and ethnic make-up, a powerful *alteño* identity has emerged there. Though some of the developments of recent years have revealed traits that militate against grassroots mobilization, there are also important ones that push in the other direction. The fact that there has been something of a lull in popular mobilization in recent years does not mean that this will always be the case. The continuing growth of El Alto, and with it the demands of its people for basic services and employment, will place strain on governments – central and local – in the future. The willingness of these to respond will depend, to a large extent, on demands emanating from the grass roots. Since it remains a highly organized society, El Alto will be capable of exerting considerable pressure on the state. This degree of organization is not static. It varies greatly according to political circumstances. That it has become atomized in recent years does not preclude the potential for collective action across the city. Few had predicted the situation that had built up in 2003 and the sort of response that resulted. Such situations could repeat themselves if and when governments in La Paz palpably fail to take account of the needs and interests of those living above them in El Alto, and new leaderships emerge that reflect deep dissatisfaction within society.

4 | OF MINES AND MINERS

The department of Potosí in south-western Bolivia and its capital city of the same name are synonymous with mining, both past and present. It was the discovery of the Cerro Rico in 1545, a brick-red conical former volcano that overshadows the city of Potosí, which provided the nexus between what was to become Bolivia and Spain for nearly three hundred years. Indeed, the name Potosí is derived from the mountain, *potochi* being the Quechua for 'exploded'. The term *'vale un Potosí'* in Spain means 'worth a fortune'. It was not the first silver mine that the Spanish discovered – this was Porco, near Potosí, a mine still in production – but Potosí was to become by far the world's main source of silver well into the nineteenth century. Of all the silver that was shipped to Spain during the colonial period, around half came from Potosí, 30 per cent from Mexico and the remaining 20 per cent from a variety of other sources in the Americas. Between coin and silver ingots, it is reckoned that some twenty billion tons of silver were dispatched by mule to Callao and thence to Cadiz via Portobello (Panama) and Havana (Cuba). The coin from Potosí, which was valid tender throughout the Spanish empire and which helped fund the Spanish monarchy's predilection for warfare in Europe, bore a unique stamp, 'pts', to denote its place of origin. Much of this wealth also made its way into the coffers of England and Holland, boosting them in turn as imperial powers.

During the colonial period, Potosí was one of the richest cities in the Americas, if not in the world. Today the department is the poorest part of the poorest country in South America. The mining industry in Potosí, and its extreme volatility due to fluctuations in price and the supply of minerals, is a good example of the 'resource curse'. The Cerro Rico is still the main source of employment in the town – employing four out of every ten workers – but the returns on the labour invested in eking out a living from its network of largely exhausted seams is meagre indeed. The largest company in the city,

Manquiri, in coordination with mining cooperatives, dedicates itself to the processing of the tailings from nearly five hundred years of continuous exploitation. The mountain itself is partly caving in, undermined by the hundreds of tunnels and galleries within, still worked by miners from the cooperatives. There is a UNESCO project to underpin the peak of the mountain with a concrete base and lightweight fillings to stop it falling in any further. Despite its poverty, Potosí is a world heritage site, and the conical mountain is its symbol to the world outside.

The tide of Potosí's fortunes turned well before supplies of readily available silver began to run out. At the beginning of the twentieth century, following the development of the armaments industry and such humdrum inventions as the hermetically sealed tin can, tin overtook silver as Bolivia's main contribution to the global economy. The boom in tin mining, centred mainly in the north of Potosí and nearby provinces in the department of Oruro, led to the development of new centres of production, principally in and around the towns of Uncía and Llallagua. The biggest of these was Siglo XX, owned by Simón Patiño. Tin mining brought a new source of wealth to Bolivia, or at least to a trio of mine owners, who became known as the 'tin barons'. These accumulated vast fortunes; at the time he died Patiño, the only Bolivian to create a global business empire, was one of the world's wealthiest individuals. However, little of his wealth, or those of other mining dynasties like the Aramayos and the Hochschilds, trickled down to benefit their countrymen, still less those that laboured for them in the mines. Until their political power began to be challenged in the late 1930s – partly by nascent mining trade unions – and their mines were subsequently nationalized in 1952, the state in Bolivia, dominated by a small group known as the 'rosca' (literally a closed circle), worked largely to further their business interests.

The decline of the Bolivian tin industry was already in evidence well before nationalization. The most valuable seams had been worked out by 1952, and the quality of the ores mined was in sharp decline by that time. Tin prices, boosted by wars, proved very volatile. Meanwhile, other producing countries – notably Malaysia, Indonesia and more recently Brazil – used open-cast techniques rather than deep mining and were able to produce tin more cheaply than Bolivia.

Strapped for investment cash, successive Bolivian governments failed to invest in the mining industry, particularly in exploration for new sources of minerals. Rather, funds were squeezed out of the mining industry and redirected towards financing agribusiness in the eastern lowlands, particularly in Santa Cruz. The *coup de grâce* for the Bolivian mining industry came in 1985, at the time of the collapse of tin prices on the London Metal Exchange. The government of Víctor Paz Estenssoro, the very man who had nationalized the mines in 1952, set about the closure of the tin industry, at least that part of it which was in state hands. Some 27,000 mineworkers lost their jobs as a result of closure and what euphemistically became known as '*relocalización*' (relocation). They included 5,000 workers from Siglo XX and the nearby concentration plant at Catavi. Private sector mines took the best of the pickings and the rest were handed over to mining cooperatives. Prime among the private sector mines were those of Comsur, owned by Bolivia's richest individual at the time and the architect of the Paz government's economic policies, Gonzalo Sánchez de Lozada, who in 1993 became president.

The period since 2007, however, has seen something of a reversal in Potosí's ebbing fortunes, and that of the Bolivian mining industry as a whole. The revival in world prices for commodities such as tin and silver, but also others such as zinc, gold and lead, has helped resuscitate mining operations in Potosí and other mining departments such as La Paz and Oruro. Mines that were largely abandoned in the 1980s became sites of feverish activity as mining once again became a profitable activity. The case of Siglo XX stands out. It provides employment for at least as many miners as those displaced in the 1980s, working in cooperatives and selling what they can produce to intermediaries. But, as we shall see, they enjoy none of the rights painstakingly won by the mineworkers' union (FSTMB), a much-diminished force since 1985. They work with neither the benefits of mechanization nor proper ventilation in the mine. And although their incomes have risen along with the rise in mineral prices, working conditions are more akin to those of the sixteenth century, not those of the twentieth, still less the twenty-first. As the FSTMB's general secretary, David Ramos, told us: 'things have changed little from colonial times'.

Changes in structure

The tin crisis of the early 1980s, the change of government in 1985 and the adoption of neoliberal policies thereafter brought dramatic changes to the shape of Bolivian mining. The closure of almost all the mining operations nationalized in 1952 caused – as we have seen – the dismissal of large cohorts of mineworkers. The Corporación Minera de Bolivia (Comibol), the state mining company created in 1952, became a shell entity without any real purpose other than to sign contracts with other firms. The closure of the mines and the subsequent *relocalización* of workers also brought the once combative FSTMB, founded in 1944, to its knees. It was the mining unions which had managed, through constant pressure on the government and Comibol, to extend workers' rights in the mines, even though such rights were always fairly basic. The knock-on effect on the Bolivian union movement and the Central Obrera Boliviana (COB) was profound, with labour-based organization much weakened thereafter.

Nowhere did the change in policy have such an impact as in Siglo XX, hitherto the largest tin mine in the country, and its surrounding communities. As a result of *relocalización*, the workforce at Siglo XX was reduced from 5,000 to a rump of 400, who refused all incentives to move them. Among them was Basilio Oporto, who still lives in a two-roomed miner's terrace house in Siglo XX. 'They weren't able to move us; we resisted,' he says proudly. Almost all miners at the time lived in tied accommodation, which meant that as soon as they lost their jobs, they lost their homes too. The company store (*pulpería*), which made food available to the miners and their families, was closed down, alongside medical services and schools previously provided by Comibol. Trucks were made available to transport workers elsewhere. Finally, in an attempt to shift the four hundred or so who refused to go (many for ideological reasons), in 1993 the government offered them the equivalent of US$1,000 to leave. 'It was savage,' recalls José Pimentel, a national union leader at the time who went on to become minister of mines under the MAS government. According to Tomás Quiroz, also previously a national union leader who is currently the mayor of Llallagua, the town adjacent to the mine, 'Paz Estenssoro wanted to close down the mining industry [...] we managed to maintain a presence here through the cooperatives.' However, the impact was felt not just by the miners and their families but by the whole community. Llallagua saw its population reduced to around 20,000 from some 35,000 prior to *relocalización*, its commerce hit by the removal of the one industry that brought money into the area. The rural communities of Norte Potosí saw the market for their produce disappear.

The closure of most of the state mining sector saw the rapid expansion of 'cooperative' mining. There had been small mines run as cooperatives before then, and the Federación de Cooperativas Mineras (Fencomin) had represented them at a national level since the 1960s. On the fringes of the industry, there were also other kinds of organization (*locatarios*, *lameros*) working seams that larger organizations were no longer prepared to exploit, using rudimentary technologies and often working in very unsafe conditions. In 1985 and subsequent years, anyone wanting to continue working in mining – apart from the bigger companies – had to constitute a cooperative. They took over many of the mines abandoned by Comibol, along with the machinery available and the houses abandoned by the unionized workforce. But without capital to invest, the machinery soon broke down. Much of it was also vandalized or sold off to make a quick buck. As we shall see, mining cooperatives were often cooperative in name, not in fact. They tended to be organizations of associates, working for themselves, for immediate profit, day to day, without any consideration for the longer term. However, they provided a basic livelihood for people in the areas left vacant by the state, and many of the '*cooperativistas*' maintained a dual existence between agricultural activities and those of the mine. As with Siglo XX, it was only after 1985 that in Potosí cooperatives began to multiply, though some date back several decades. There are at least fifty cooperatives involved in mining the Cerro Rico for the last vestiges of its silver wealth, employing around 15,000 workers. All told, there are four federations of cooperatives in the department of Potosí, in the north (Llallagua), the centre (Potosí), the south-west (Uyuni) and the south (Atocha).

The demise of the state sector also saw the consolidation of the private sector. Known traditionally as the *minería mediana*, in fact this sector represents the largest firms in Bolivia as well as some of the smaller. The private sector accounts for more than 60 per cent of production, but employs less than 10 per cent of the workforce. It thus represents the highly capitalized portion of the industry. In a sense, Bolivia has seen the development of a dualist mining industry: a private sector in which productivity is very high, and a cooperative sector in which it is extremely low. Many of the main private companies took over parts of Comibol where ore grades were still reasonably high. They included Sinchi Wayra (Glencore, previously Comsur), Pan-American Silver (San Vicente) and Manquiri (San Bartolomé). But the giant in the sector is San Cristóbal, in south-western Potosí, worked by Japan's Sumitomo. This is a new mine, although it took over an existing one. Work on San Cristóbal began in 1996, with production starting up in 2007. It works mainly zinc-silver and lead-silver deposits, and since it began output, silver and zinc have taken over as Bolivia's two most important mining exports. Tin, the mainstay of the Bolivian economy for the best part of a century, is now fourth in order of importance. San Cristóbal apart, there has been little private investment in the Bolivian mining industry, particularly compared with neighbouring Chile and Peru. According to the Private Miners' Association (Asociación de Minería Mediana), the problem lies with the lack of a stable outlook for the sector, and in particular with the tax regime. 'We want rules that provide proper incentives for investment,' says Gerardo Garrett of Minera San Cristóbal, 'we want guarantees and legal security.' But even under the Sánchez de Lozada government and its immediate successors, there was virtually no investment, despite the enormous geological potential the country offers.

A further change in the structure of mining is more recent. Under Evo Morales and the MAS, since 2006 the public sector has re-entered the business as an actor, having been all but shut out for the previous two decades. The resuscitation of Comibol – as a key planner in the sector, as the owner of important subsoil resources, as a partner with a number of private sector concerns, as promoter of industrialization, and as a producer in its own right – has brought the state back into the picture. So far as its role as a producer is concerned, its main mining operation is at Huanuni in the department of Oruro, the only large tin mine still left in operation. Huanuni had been privatized to a British firm, but following a series of bankruptcies it was reacquired by the state in 2006. Since then, and following some essential investment, production at the mine more than doubled by 2011. With the construction of a new refinery there, production should continue to increase. The other significant mine owned by Comibol is Corocoro in La Paz department, one of Bolivia's few sites of copper production. In June 2012, after an attempt by cooperative miners to take over the mine, Colquiri – also in La Paz – was renationalized, taking to three the number of state-operated mines. But the role of Comibol seems set to expand into new areas, particularly in the production of non-traditional minerals and the industrialization of minerals produced. Like Huanuni, the tin smelter at Vinto, just outside Oruro, has returned to state ownership, and at the time of writing Comibol was involved in trying to resurrect the Karachipampa, a silver and lead smelter just outside Potosí city, a project started and then mothballed in the 1970s.

Also at the time of writing, Bolivia was awaiting the passage of a new Mining Law, designed to bring the legal framework for the industry into line with the 2009 constitution. This would involve changes in private sector contracts with the state. It would also involve changes in taxation. The Morales government had already raised taxes payable by private companies by increasing taxes on profits to reflect the increase in mineral prices (to 37.5 per cent) , as well as reintroducing royalty payments on production. The issue of taxation had been left to last in discussions over the Mining Law, with Gerardo Garrett from Minera San Cristóbal foreseeing a 'big battle' in the offing. Prior to the Morales government, the private sector mining companies had contributed relatively little to the public coffers. Another point of friction with regard to tax was the contribution of cooperative miners to the treasury. Hitherto, at least, cooperatives had contributed virtually nothing by way of tax, and this seemed likely to be a source of future friction between the government and the large number of mineworkers operating in this sector.

The workings of cooperatives

As we have seen, the vast majority of workers in the mining sector in Bolivia today belong to cooperatives. These vary greatly in size. One of the largest cooperatives is the Cooperativa Minera Unificada, which is among those involved in extracting what remains of the mineral contained in the Cerro Rico in Potosí. This has 3,000 associates (who technically 'own' the cooperative) plus a further 2,000 who work as labourers and are hired on a daily basis. But most cooperatives are much smaller than this, and more precarious as business entities. To become a cooperative, you need to have as few as ten associates. The 'associates' are, to a large extent, individual operators, hiring and firing daily labourers as they (and the market) see fit.

In Potosí, Siglo XX and elsewhere, the numbers of cooperatives expanded hugely with the rise in mineral prices. 'They popped up like mushrooms,' says Tomás Quiroz, the mayor of Llallagua who was previously the vice-minister responsible for cooperatives at the beginning of the Morales government.

Cooperatives operate on their own, with little or no outside over-sight – although they are supposed to obey their own statutes. Their members give a proportion of the value of the mineral they produce to the cooperative to cover administrative expenses and other costs they might have to incur. Workers labour either individually or in groups (*cuadrillas* of up to one hundred people), but unlike in formal mining enterprises they do not work to fixed timetables. Individual associates turn up when they like and leave when they like, although in practice most work long hours underground. At Siglo XX, for instance, miners have to walk as far as 3 kilometres before they reach a seam they can exploit, and then have to return the same distance carrying the ore they have mined on their backs. Remuneration is by the quantity (and quality) of what is mined, not the time spent underground. The extent to which they generate money for themselves also depends on the amount of rock that needs to be cleared within the mine before access to the seam is gained. Investment in safety and in the search for new seams is work that is not remunerated.

The degree of democracy and participation in a cooperative also varies widely. In the more institutionalized cooperatives, meetings are held reasonably regularly – albeit not necessarily on fixed schedules. Transparency in the way a cooperative is managed is also dependent on whether such meetings take place regularly and whether leaders are held to account. The Multiactiva cooperative at Catavi, which works the tailings from Siglo XX, is one of the more highly institutionalized and one of the few that works to cooperative principles. According to Basilio Oporto, one of the founders of the Multiactiva, meetings take place regularly at different levels – meetings of directors, *ampliados* (plenary meetings) and general assemblies – but when required. 'Our organization is the best here [in Siglo XX],' he says; 'we impose a system of penalties for infractions and kick out those people who steal [from the cooperative].'

As mineral prices have risen, the economic fortunes of cooperatives have improved, as have the wage rates paid to workers for what they produce. Associates sell their produce to dealers who sell the ore on to other intermediaries in a chain of commercialization. At the small end of the chain are the *rescatistas* (small-scale intermediaries), who buy at around 50 per cent of the value of the ore. Most of them seem to be aware that the traders they sell to tend to cheat them and give them less than they ought for their production. But unless they can trade together and in bulk, it is difficult to drive a hard bargain. According to Artemio Mamani, president of the Regional Federation of Cooperative Miners of North Potosí (Ferecominorpo), for most 'there is no alternative but to sell to the intermediaries'. Attempts have been made to use the cooperatives to pool production and then sell direct, but these have not proved successful. 'To do this you need to be able to count on credit, at least one million bolivianos,' says Mamani, 'and there are those who stand to lose [like the *rescatistas*] who are opposed and therefore make life difficult.' In the opinion of Benito Ramos Callisaya, now a national deputy who worked as a miner from his boyhood in Potosí, 'the ideal would be for the state to set up an agency to buy mineral from the *cooperativistas*'. At least for those working in and around Potosí, the implementation of the Karachipampa project would be a major help.

The most pressing problem facing the cooperative sector is the chronic lack of investment in the mines. Although some of the better-organized cooperatives, such as the Multiactiva, have been able to invest in machinery and vehicles to transport ore, this is not the case with the vast majority of cooperatives, which live day to day without much thought for the future. The appalling working conditions at Siglo XX stand as a monument to the lack of any investment, either in productive machinery or in health and safety. As we have seen, time spent in propping up the shafts or in digging new ventilation shafts is time that is not remunerated. 'They prefer not to invest,' says Benito Ramos. According to Quiroz, the *cooperativista*s prefer to spend what they earn on 'cars, motorbikes and housing', not on investing in the future of the mine. Ramos goes on to say that 'industrial safety is our main weakness' and that it is down to the *dirigentes* of the cooperative 'to undertake permanent checks'. At Siglo XX industrial accidents are common, not least because of faulty electrical equipment within the mine installed over thirty years ago. According to Artemio Mamani of Ferecominorpo, the problem is that the mineral that is easiest to extract has now all been worked out, and miners are obliged to work in galleries that are ever more marginal and dangerous. Often the only access to a seam is by crawling through narrow reaches, with virtually no ventilation.

Ultimately, the viability of the cooperative sector is entirely dependent on the maintenance of high mineral prices in international markets. 'If the price collapses', says Mamani, 'it will be like 1984–86 all over again.' Gerardo Garrett at Minera San Cristóbal agrees. 'If prices fall, they [the cooperatives] will cease to be. Where will all these people find alternative work?'

However, as a result of buoyant mineral prices, living standards appear to have improved over the last few years. In 2003, for instance, the price of silver was around US$5 a troy ounce, while in recent times it has risen briefly as far as US$49. Wages within the Cooperativa Unificada have risen as a result. According to Benito Ramos, a worker in the Cerro Rico could expect to earn 120 bolivianos (around US$17) a day in 2012. The going rate in 2003–05 was around 40 bolivianos. Back in 1994, when prices were rock bottom, the rate would have been about 16 bolivianos. At the Cooperativa Multiactiva in Catavi, the average monthly wage was about 2,200 bolivianos (around US$315) a month in 2012. 'We've managed to improve a lot on what we pay,' says Basilio Oporto, pointing to a 7 per cent rise in 2011. The rise in prices has also led to large increases in the numbers involved in mining cooperatives. The flow of new migrants from rural areas into the town of Llallagua has been particularly strong, with new neighbourhoods springing into existence, creating further demand for basic services like electricity, water and sewerage. 'When the prices [of minerals] go up, people from rural areas come to live in the town,' says Quiroz, the mayor of Llallagua; 'the problem for us is that they demand more than they contribute [in local taxes].' However, he also points to a sharp increase in the amount of savings in credit unions and other savings and loans organizations as evidence of increased prosperity.

The pace of urban growth is also very much in evidence in Potosí, where new neighbourhoods have sprung up in the last five years. In both towns, the minerals boom has led to a large expansion in commercial activity. In Llallagua this has been further encouraged by the expansion of numbers of students enrolled at the University of Siglo XX, a project dating from the 1980s set up at the insistence of the national miners' union (FSTMB) and with its active participation. At the same time, the increased flow of money has had negative effects. According to Dora Villanueva, who has been actively involved in community affairs in Potosí, there has been a marked increase in alcoholism, intra-familial violence and the appearance of brothels in the city. Problems of alcoholism are also common in Llallagua, a town with a large youthful population. When asked what *'vivir bien'* meant for cooperative miners, Artemio Mamani responded, 'it means work, to be earning money, to be able to buy food and drink'.

Those we interviewed in Siglo XX and in Potosí pointed to many tangible improvements brought about by the MAS government since 2006. In the elections of both 2005 and 2009, Potosí was one of the departments where the victory of the MAS was most overwhelming. Mineworkers, whether working in cooperatives or in other types of mining operation, had been hugely supportive of Morales and the MAS. The main exception here was the cooperatives of central and southern Potosí, which had tended to side with right-wing parties in the 2005 elections. 'We the *cooperativistas* backed the MAS and the *proceso de cambio* [process of change],' says Benito Ramos, 'and we had huge hopes of Evo.' In his first administration, at least at the beginning, Morales rewarded the *cooperativistas* by appointing one of their number, Wálter Villaroel, as mining minister with a seat in the cabinet. The role of cooperatives more generally was ratified by the creation of a vice-ministry for cooperatives within the Ministry of Labour, a post previously held by Tomás Quiroz.

Apart from the *bonos* received by particular sectors of the population, the miners had benefited from gifts from the central government. In Siglo XX, the main cooperatives there, including the Cooperativa 20 de Octubre and the Cooperativa Siglo XX, the two largest, received mobile pneumatic compressors to improve ventilation within the mine. Not all cooperatives found these so useful; the Multiactiva Cooperative (which does not work underground) had little use for a compressor. 'We should have asked for a truck,' says Basilio Oporto. Similarly, the government has also provided small refining plants to reduce the miners' dependency on intermediaries and to raise the value of what they produce. In practice, however, this did not work as well as had been hoped. To run a refinery requires skills that the miners themselves do not possess. The refinery belonging to the Cooperativa Siglo XX had, at the time of writing, still to come into operation.

A test of the cooperatives' support for the government was due in 2012 as the new Mining Law was expected to come into effect. In the discussions surrounding the elaboration of the law, the mining cooperatives and their national organization, Fencomin, had been reluctant to give ground. They disagree with paying any form of tax and resist entering into a regime of contracts with Comibol.

Mining unions

Huanuni, situated between Oruro and Llallagua, is Bolivia's largest functioning tin mine. Unlike Siglo XX and many other mining centres that had previously been in the state sector, Huanuni escaped closure in the mid- to late 1980s. Given its high-quality ore and its relatively low operating costs, it was considered viable, even at the low world price for tin that prevailed at the time. Today, it is a relatively mechanized operation – at least when compared with most of the cooperative mines – and has undergone expansion since being returned to the state sector in 2006. Large trucks enter the mine and, about a kilometre in from the mine entrance, descend a tunnel that spirals corkscrew fashion downwards, from which galleries radiate outwards towards the drilling faces. The machinery in the mine is by no means new – much of it is at least thirty years old – but it is a far cry from the precarious conditions of Siglo XX only a few miles distant.

Up until 1987, there were some 2,500 miners working at Huanuni, all members of the FSTMB. As such it was one of the more important unionized mines. As elsewhere, the years that followed saw various attempts by governments of the time to persuade workers to 'relocate', including monetary inducements. But the mine was kept open. Although the authorities had wanted to sell it, in March 2000 it was hived off in a joint venture with Comibol at a bargain basement price to a British registered firm, Allied Deals. So at least in theory, Huanuni remained in the public sector. The mine's union members, much reduced in number, opposed the deal. Conditions in the mine deteriorated at the time and health and education facilities, previously provided by Comibol, became a thing of the past. In 2002, on the eve of presidential elections, the union linked up with the Civic Committee in Oruro in defence of the mine. Allied Deals and its successor RBG, both of which went bust, were eventually expelled from Bolivia, and the judiciary intervened. Although private interests, including Sánchez de Lozada's Comsur, had sought to get their hands on Huanuni, it was eventually handed over in its entirety to Comibol following the inauguration of the MAS government.

The role of the unionized workforce, as opposed to that of the co-operatives who had occupied part of the mine, came to public attention in October 2006. The numbers of *cooperativistas* had increased steadily with the recovery of world tin prices. By 2006, there were 4,000 cooperative miners as opposed to just 800 unionized workers. Conflict arose as the cooperative miners sought to appropriate the seams worked by the *sindicalizados*. Sixteen miners lost their lives as open conflict broke out between the two sides. In the end, the government was obliged to respond by officially hiring the 4,000 *cooperativistas* as wage workers. At the same time, Evo Morales sacked Villaroel, the then *cooperativista* minister of mines. The rift, however, took time to heal, and incorporating the *cooperativistas* has not been easy. 'The *cooperativistas* do not believe in *sindicalismo*,' says Miguel Zubieta, previously executive secretary of the FSTMB from Huanuni, but, he adds, 'the process is now irreversible'.

The high price of tin has enabled Huanuni to absorb the larger workforce and still make profits. The basic wage has increased substantially since 2006, including a bonus paid as a proportion of operating profits. According to Zubieta, wage rises are authorized only when the company is making profits. 'We raise our wages not because of what the government says, but in line with the profits the mine makes,' he says. He points out that there was no wage rise in 2010 when wages in the rest of the public sector increased by 7 per cent. 'We belong to the old generation,' he notes, 'but there is now a new generation of union leaders with a different mentality.' However, both the union and the company board – with its two worker representatives – are today playing an important part in developing a responsible attitude to state management.

But those employed in the state mining sector – basically those in Huanuni, Corocoro and Colquiri (where a similar process of incorporating cooperative miners has taken place) – represent only a small fraction of the unionized workforce. Most work in the private sector, where traditions of collective bargaining are very different. According to David Ramos, the FSTMB leader, in 1997 there were twenty active trade unions; today this number has increased to seventy, with the number of affiliates much increased. The executive committee of the FSTMB is made up of forty *dirigentes* from the private sector and only six from the public sector.

In the private sector, management exercises far more control over industrial relations. 'The private sector unions are under the thumb of the bosses,' says Zubieta, and while wages may be reasonably high, 'there is no worker participation in the running of the company'. In some cases, moreover, with modern mining companies introducing new forms of working, such as twenty-one days on-site and seven days off with families, the mining village is disappearing. This is having a fundamental effect on the sense of solidarity within mining communities and probably also on the cohesion of mining organization.

Industrialization

Unlike in the hydrocarbons sector, the policy of the Morales administration towards mining has not sought to bring the private sector under state control, except when forced to do so (as in the case of Colquiri) by local conditions. Rather it has been to extend state participation into new sectors and to focus on increasing the value-added generated through industrialization. The latter is hardly a new policy; it had been employed during governments in the 1960s and 1970s. However, it contrasts with the lack of interest in industrialization during the governments of the 1980s and 1990s, inspired by neoliberal economic principles. Various industrialization projects, by their nature capital intensive, do little to provide productive employment themselves but promise to add value substantially to exports, augment the income of the state and thereby generate funds for social welfare spending.

A number of metallurgical projects, dating from the earlier period of industrialization, have been resuscitated and given new dynamism. Chief among these has been the recovery by the state of the smelter at Vinto, just outside Oruro. This had been acquired by Sinchi Wayra, property at one stage of Sánchez de Lozada and then acquired by Glencore. In 2007 it was renationalized. Vinto, where the existing plant is at least forty years old, buys tin from Huanuni, private companies and a large number of cooperatives, adding value to the basic ore by smelting the concentrates and then exporting them. The capacity of Vinto was due to be increased substantially by 2012 with the installation of the new Ausmelt furnace, assembled for the purpose in Santa Cruz. The funding for the new furnace came from the government and was to be repaid from the increased sales it would facilitate. Similarly, the Morales government sought to revive the Karachipampa project in Potosí, to smelt lead and silver. Furthermore, two hydro-metallurgical plants were being planned in Oruro and Potosí to process zinc and silver. These will enable other minerals, currently lost because of the bulk export of ores and their processing abroad, to be refined locally.

Another project was to exploit massive reserves of iron ore in Mutún in the far south-east of Santa Cruz close to the Brazilian border. Originally, the idea was to undertake this with a Brazilian firm, but this bid was abandoned. A contract signed with Jindal of India was eventually rescinded in 2012 given lack of investment by the Indian parent company. The second half of the deposit was to be developed by the Bolivian state company, Empresa Siderúrgica del Mutún (ESM). The idea was not just to produce (and export) iron ore – which Bolivia currently imports – but to produce steel by the 2014 target date. The project encountered difficulties, including the supply of natural gas. Also the problems involved in transporting iron and steel to foreign markets proved appreciable. The idea is to ship production out on giant rafts using the Paraná–Plate river system. At the time of writing, it was unclear exactly how this potentially large project would evolve.

But the project with, potentially, the biggest implications is the development of lithium and potash production from the salt lakes of southern Oruro and western Potosí, particularly the Salar de Uyuni. The lithium project is being developed in its initial stages by Bolivia alone, with a pilot plant to produce lithium carbonate. This is due to be followed up by a plant to industrialize lithium and to increase production fifty-fold by 2016. Then finally a third phase is planned to produce cathodes of lithium, the essential item for manufacturing lithium batteries for electric cars. The value-added at this stage is very large, with a ton of cathodes selling at anything up to US$40,000 (while a ton of lithium carbonate is priced at US$4,500). An agreement has been signed with a Korean consortium, Kores Posco, to that end. Bolivia is reckoned to have the world's largest deposits of lithium in the brine that lies beneath the surface of the Salar de Uyuni. Lithium also has a potential role in nuclear fission. At the same time, the salt lakes have huge deposits of potash. These are being developed jointly with a Chinese firm that is keen to exploit this huge potential to produce fertilizers. But development of both lithium and potash has taken longer than expected. 'All this will involve a lot of good fortune,' says Alberto Echazú, the official at Comibol in charge of evaporitics (as this branch of mining is known); 'we suffer from a deadweight bureaucracy and a lack of local expertise, but we're learning fast.'

Conclusions

The potential for mining in Bolivia is enormous, despite a chronic lack of investment which has resulted in failure to identify major new sources of minerals. The attempts of the Morales government to exploit new reserves – lithium in the west and iron ore in the east – represent one of the first initiatives to expand new sources of mineral wealth. Its attempts to link these to industrialization projects should – if prices hold up – bring new sources of income to the state, which can then be redistributed to society as a whole. The Morales administration has pursued the resuscitation of state involvement in mining, and especially in metallurgy, but relations between the state, the private sector and the cooperatives remain uneasy.

However, as with the gas industry in the south-east of Bolivia, modern mining is highly capital intensive. It does not provide work for a still rapidly expanding population. New mining initiatives mean few jobs: the workforce at San Cristóbal, by far Bolivia's largest mine in terms of output, numbers only 600, while lithium production at the Salar de Uyuni involved only 150 at the time of writing. The bulk of employment within the mining industry is in the cooperative sector, where productivity is low. At the time of writing there were an estimated 80,000–100,000 *cooperativistas*. As we have seen, the Bolivian mining industry suffers from a sort of dualism: a modern, mechanized sector which accounts for the lion's share of output and exports, alongside a labour-intensive 'cooperative' sector which accounts for most of the employment generated in the sector but which is highly vulnerable to cyclical downturns in the market price for minerals. High prices in recent years have led to the creation of more jobs, but a sharp downturn could have disastrous consequences.

The cooperative sector has gained significant political power under the Morales administration, providing an important source of support for the government. Up to 100,000 people are involved, mainly youngsters, and this number far exceeds that of those who work in unionized mines, in both the public and private sectors. The support of the *cooperativistas* is not unconditional, however; they remain assertive political actors in defence of their own perceived interests, which are essentially short-term and lack much by way of vision. Although they employ large numbers of workers, they do not allow these to become unionized. Nor do they pay taxes or (in most instances) invest in increasing potential output. Indeed, as we have seen, they have found themselves at loggerheads with the *sindicalizados*, competing for control over strategically significant seams of ore. For David Ramos, at the FSTMB, the associates of the cooperative movement represent the 'new *criollo* bourgeoisie' of the mining industry. They have many of the characteristics of private companies.

The example provided by Huanuni, where the *cooperativistas* were absorbed into the unionized workforce (and saw their working conditions and living standards improve as a result), has been copied at Colquiri. An increased role for Comibol may provide greater stability in employment in the industry, but Comibol is likewise not immune from the vagaries of the international market. The Morales government has seen a recovery in the strength of the unionized sector of the industry, albeit from a low ebb. However, the FSTMB is far from regaining its previous leadership role among social movements. The number of FSTMB members is much higher from the private than from the state sector. Fissures in worker organization therefore remain.

Meanwhile, increases in taxation – for many years the industry paid very little to the Treasury – may at least help socialize some of the benefits of the industry. For the private sector, however, such increases were anathema, as they were to the *cooperativistas*. As discussions over a new Ley Minera reached a climax in 2012, disagreements about the roles and responsibilities of mining companies (particularly with respect to the payment of tax) seemed unlikely to establish a new consensus between private entrepreneurs, workers and the state.

5 | OF COCA AND *COCALEROS*

Shinahota is a down-at-heel town on the main road through the Chapare that connects Santa Cruz and Cochabamba. Huge trucks roar past, the road providing the commercial connection between the towns and cities of the Oriente and those of the valleys and highlands to the west. It is therefore strategically located. Despite its appearance, it is a town with evident signs of wealth. Youngsters whizz around on motorbikes imported from China. Large, powerful jeeps are parked on the main street, many without number plates (indicating that they have probably been imported illegally). Satellite dishes sprout from the roofs of every building in sight, indicating that this is a town where people are highly connected with the outside world. Such is the acquisitive power of people in this part of the Chapare that merchants from Santa Cruz, 300 kilometres away, come here to sell their goods in the Sunday market. It is a town that has grown rapidly since the 1980s, when it consisted of a few shacks along the highway. The main source of wealth in this area is coca.

Two kilometres down the road from Shinahota is Lauca Ñ. Out of the steamy banana plantations and up a bumpy track appears a large three-storey building, painted orange and with the polarized, reflective windows that are so much in fashion in today's Bolivia. This is the headquarters of the Seis Federaciones, the six coca federations of the Chapare, whose president is Evo Morales. It was here in 2002 that Morales was chosen as presidential candidate for his party, the Movimiento al Socialismo (MAS). The orange-coloured building also houses the offices and studio of Radio Kawsachun Coca (Viva Coca), which broadcasts to the entire Chapare region. Its motto is '*la revolución que se escucha*' (the revolution that is listened to). Next door is a large multi-purpose sporting arena, covered by a curved corrugated-iron roof with the appearance of an airport hangar, where, when we arrived, an important meeting was taking place.

Inside, a thousand or so delegates were assembling from across the region for an emergency meeting (*ampliado*). They arrived from as far away as 80 kilometres, struggling up from the main road under plastic sheets to protect them from the torrential rain. In previous days, in Cochabamba city, the offices of the Federación del Trópico, one of the six federations (and the one from which Morales hails), had had its windows broken by medical students supporting striking doctors, who had hurled rocks from the street. The meeting was to last all day, with delegates from each of the six federations listening attentively to their *dirigentes* and then voting among themselves as to how best to respond. They decided the best thing to do was to stage a large demonstration on the streets of Cochabamba, with a view to reminding local opinion there of their determination to support their president and his government. The coca farmers are a force to be reckoned with, both locally and in the country as a whole.

The *cocaleros* of the Chapare occupy a very special place in the politics of Morales's Bolivia. Not only is their leader the president of the country but they hold him accountable for what goes on in government. They are highly organized and the leaders of the six federations have a direct and – as the conclave we witnessed in Lauca Ñ showed – constant and fluid relationship with their grass-roots members. The model of organization is one that has adapted itself from the traditional models of agrarian syndicalism in Bolivia, but with a strong dose of experience of militant politics derived from the country's miners and their union tradition. Some miners settled in the Chapare in the 1980s, when the mines were closed down, but the organization of the mineworkers had long impacted on rural unions here and elsewhere. The federations are powerful organizations locally, influencing in very direct form the distribution of landholding among members. It is impossible to hold land or to be a coca farmer without being a member of the union. And, as repeated electoral results have shown, this is a bastion of the MAS, where participation in elections is high and where preference for the ruling party and its candidate is almost universal. Unlike other parts of Bolivia, this is not a place where you hear much criticism about the government of Evo Morales.

The war on coca

Although coca has been grown in Bolivia and other Andean coun-tries since time immemorial, attempts to control coca production began in earnest only in the 1980s. With the beginnings of mass consumption of cocaine as a recreational drug in developed countries (principally in the United States), the 1970s had seen the growth of drug trafficking mafias in Bolivia, and in particular in Santa Cruz. The emergence of luxurious neighbourhoods like Equipetrol in Santa Cruz city bore witness to the wealth being created at this time from drug trafficking during the Banzer dictatorship (1971–78) and afterwards. The rapid expansion in the number of high-rise buildings in La Paz was also, at least in part, a symptom of the need to launder the money generated by the nascent cocaine industry. Internationally, Bolivia became conspicuous with the 'cocaine' coup of 1980, when a group of military officers working in cahoots with drug interests from Santa Cruz and elsewhere seized power, deposing the interim civilian government of President Lidia Gueiler, Bolivia's first woman president. The García Meza coup, alongside the offers of drug lord Roberto Suárez to pay off Bolivia's foreign debt from his personal fortune, caught the attention of the administration in Washington. Instead of the spread of international communism – a fixation of US policy towards Bolivia since 1952 – drugs became the predominant issue in bilateral relations.

Traditionally coca had been grown in the Yungas, the steep-sided valleys stretching down from the Andes in the department of La Paz towards the Amazon jungle lowlands. Its main use was for coca chewing (known in Bolivia as *acullico* or *pijcheo*), practised to ward off the effects of hunger and fatigue, but also an important element in traditional cultural and religious rituals. The trade in coca between the Yungas and the Altiplano goes back to pre-Columbian times. Today, the main growing areas are around the towns of Coroico, Coripata, Chulumani and Irupana and, slightly farther north, around La Asunta. The growth of the Chapare as a source of supply dated from the 1970s, a result of the increase in drug demand on the one hand and a massive influx of agricultural and other workers from highland Bolivia under government-sponsored colonization schemes on the other. The area had first been opened up for colonization and thus coca growing by the construction of a road in the 1960s from the city of Cochabamba to Villa Tunari in the tropics. Ironically, the road had been designed and funded by USAID. The coca-producing area runs east–west, parallel to the Andean foothills, stretching from the borders of Beni department in the west through to the fringes of Santa Cruz in the east.

The 'war on coca' began in a relatively desultory fashion, with US aid focused on the training of military cadres progressively to eradicate coca plants while seeking to provide monetary and other incentives for alternative development schemes through crop substitution. This 'carrot and stick' approach to coca cultivation had little impact in practice. Substitution programmes, also fostered by the European Union, failed to stem the increased number of hectares planted with coca. For the migrant farmers who had settled in the Chapare, coca had a number of very considerable advantages over other crops. Prices were generally far in excess of those for substitute crops (such as coffee or citrus fruit); coca proved a very hardy plant, resistant to many of the diseases that afflicted other tropical produce; and because it could be harvested three or four times a year (and even five in some places), it was a source of constant income for those producing it. Of course, Chapare coca farmers, or *cocaleros*, cultivated other crops both for their own consumption and for sale in the market, but as the 1980s progressed, coca became the dominant source of family income in the area.

Militarization of the Chapare region, designed to enforce eradication programmes, intensified during the course of the 1990s. It peaked during the second Banzer presidency (1997–2001) with the passage of new, more draconian legislation (Law 1008) and the enunciation of the 'zero coca' policy. Banzer and his advisers, aided and abetted by the US embassy in La Paz, set out to eradicate coca as a crop in Bolivia. Indeed, they promised to eradicate coca production in just five years. 'Carrot and stick' became simply 'stick'. The war on drugs, in Bolivia and in other producer countries, sought to prioritize the elimination at source of the raw material for cocaine, the coca bush. As such, it became a war not just against coca but against those who produce it. As Juanita Ancieta, the coordinator of the six federations, described it, 'the policy of the empire, the United States, was not just to eliminate coca but to eliminate *cocaleros* too'.

Forced eradication of coca brought the *cocaleros* into direct confrontation with the state, and particularly with the military, which was charged with implementing the 'zero coca' policy. In the words of Asterio Romero, a *cocalero dirigente* at the time (and when we interviewed him a top official in the regional government of Cochabamba department), it was the 'repression that ended up strengthening us [...] the more they tried to suppress us, the stronger we became'. Leonilda Zurita, a woman *cocalera dirigente* who was to become a senior figure in the MAS, recounted how 'we spent months on end with *bloqueos*, fighting for our rights [...] we faced the army, we faced the helicopters which shot at us from the sky [...] but we managed to resist the eradication of coca'. Mario Castillo, who migrated to the Chapare in the late 1980s from his native Chuquisaca, recalled that the military and police had 'no respect for us as a people or our human rights'. He recounts how women were routinely subject to abuse and rape. 'There was no respect, even for the more respectable-looking people,' he claims; 'it was not a good idea to go round with smart clothes or a new bicycle since they would say you must be a drug dealer, and then often end up stealing your things.'

The political organization of the *cocaleros* was therefore reinforced by the experience of resistance to the 'war on drugs'. Forceful leaders like Evo Morales rose to positions of leadership through the ranks of the union movement. For Romero, the struggle helped forge a unity between leaders and the grass roots: 'they take decisions in conjunction with the *bases* [...] but it is vital to strengthen *base*-level participation in decision-making so as to offset any weaknesses of the leadership'. Resistance to coca eradication policies also involved women, and helped break down the tendency for men to dominate the political scene. According to Elizabeth Yucra, a *dirigente* from the Tupac Katari Federation in the Chapare, 'previously we were constantly persecuted, but as women we were always out in front on the *bloqueos*'. For Faustina Casillas, a member of the executive committee of the Federación del Trópico, 'we were in permanent struggle under successive governments [...] We have experienced very personally what union life entails.' Partly because of the growing power of the MAS in national politics – after the 2002 elections it became the second-largest party grouping in the Congress – the ferocity of the 'zero coca' programme began to ebb, particularly after the resignation of Banzer on health grounds in 2001. It is also worth noting that a 'zero coca' policy, if successful, would mean a 'zero aid' policy on the part of the United States; some coca was necessary to keep the funds flowing. As Evo Morales, the president of the Federación del Trópico, became a national political figure, he was able to use his bargaining power to force the government to abandon the military offensive. As a consequence, respect for human rights in the Chapare was gradually restored.

The role played by the various federations of the Chapare had a major impact on the degree of politicization achieved among the *cocaleros*. In many respects, the *cocaleros* emerged as a new vanguard, much as the miners had been prior to 1985. 'We act as a school, or even a university,' notes Segundina Orellana, a leader of the *cocaleros* from Mariscal Sucre B and a key figure within the Federación del Trópico; 'the Federación does its own educational work [...] we are strengthening our organization every day that passes'. The emergence of the MAS as a 'political instrument' of the *cocaleros* in the late 1990s resulted from a recognition that as a social movement they had to fight both on the political terrain and as an agrarian union.

Communications, particularly radio, played a key role in facilitating coordination across the Chapare between the various federations and between the leaders and their grassroots supporters. On a previous visit to the region, in 2004, we saw how vulnerable radio installations were to attack. Radio Soberanía, a radio station located just outside Villa Tunari, had been the target of repeated assaults by the army. Today, Radio Kawsachun Coca, from its gleaming offices in Lauca Ñ, broadcasts to the whole Chapare region, to the 50,000 or so *cocaleros* as well as to the inhabitants of rapidly developing urban centres like Shinahota, Chimoré and Villa Tunari. 'We reflect the voice of the leaders and *bases* of the *cocaleros*, to provide them with the means of making their point of view heard,' says José Luis Colque, the radio's manager for the last four years. For Israel Barrenechea, who came from La Paz three years ago to work as the radio's announcer and who has got to know the region intimately in this time, 'the radio is a social instrument of organization and mobilization'. The mobile phone has also played an important role in communications over recent years.

Another important ingredient in local organization is the link-up between the federations and local government. As well as the six federations, the region is divided up into five municipalities. Since the late 1990s, these have all been controlled by the MAS. With increased budgets to municipalities generally, given the monies collected from the tax on gas production (IDH), services, at least in urban areas, have improved greatly, encouraging some coca producers to set up small shops in their 'second homes' in the towns.

Trends in coca production

Calculating how much coca is produced each year is fraught with difficulties. Often coca is grown on very small plots or under the shade of other vegetation so that plantations do not show up on aerial photography. Often, too, it is grown on very steep slopes. Nor does aerial photography take account of large variations of yields between one area and another; other forms of on-site measurement are thus required. Probably the most reliable source is the data published annually by the United Nations Office on Drugs and Crime (UNODC). The US State Department also publishes figures annually as part of its monitoring of countries and their compliance with the 'war on drugs'. These vary considerably from those of the UN, and have been used in recent years to justify Bolivia's being singled out – along with Venezuela and Burma – as 'demonstrably failing' to collaborate with US drug policy worldwide. The difficulties in coming up with accurate measurements are acknowledged in the UNODC's annual *World Drug Report*; still, it provides a useful proxy for measuring trends over time.

A starting point for estimating coca cultivation is the number of hectares planted with coca. The UN figures indicate that plantings in Bolivia fell quite dramatically in the late 1990s as a result of the Banzer government's zero coca policy. This decline was arrested in the early years of the new millennium, and since then the number of hectares has risen – though not dramatically. In 2006, the year that Evo Morales became president, there were 27,500 hectares of coca. In 2010, this had risen to 31,000 hectares. Then in 2011 (the last year for which figures were available), acreages declined significantly to 27,200 hectares. By contrast with Bolivia, acreages of coca in neighbouring Peru rose considerably faster over this time-span, but Peru (which has been less critical of Washington and its policies) avoided the opprobrium heaped on Bolivia. Of the total number of hectares planted, roughly two-thirds were in the Yungas region of La Paz, and the other third was in the Chapare.

Coca yields are more complicated to quantify than plantings. Yields vary according to altitude, with the highest yields registered for districts between 300 and 1,000 metres above sea level. In Bolivia, most coca is grown at between 1,000 and 2,000 metres. The yields in the Chapare, which is mostly considerably lower in altitude than the coca-growing districts of La Paz, are generally greater. The productive potential of the two areas is roughly similar, even though the number of hectares planted is much higher in the Yungas. According to a reckoning carried out in 2005, both regions had a productive potential of 27,000–28,000 metric tons (mt) of coca leaves. Of the total, a larger proportion of dried leaf from the Yungas is sold in the authorized market than was the case in the Chapare. Traditionally, Yungas coca provides for a larger slice of the domestic market than is the case in the Chapare, where a greater proportion is siphoned off for the manufacture of cocaine. Whereas Yungas coca is mainly grown on terraces in the Andean foothills, plantations in the Chapare are relatively flat. They tend to require less maintenance and are easier to harvest. The quality also varies; Yungas coca is in much greater demand for traditional use (*acullico*).

Public policy towards coca growing in Bolivia underwent a significant shift in the first five years of the new millennium. With the growing importance of the MAS as a political force in national politics – particularly after the 2002 elections – the policy of 'zero coca' was largely abandoned in favour of a more permissive one. The number of hectares eradicated each year declined from a peak of 15,000 in 1999 to 6,000 in 2005. When it took office in 2006, the Morales government opted for a policy of allowing individual families to cultivate a '*cato*' of coca. A *cato* is an area of 1,600 square metres, usually square in shape (40 metres by 40 metres), an area roughly the size of a basketball pitch. Failure to abide by this restriction results in sanctions by one of the local coca federations, and even expulsion from the land. As Leonilda Zurita observes, 'respect for the *cato* system is exercised through social control; we mobilize ourselves to this end'. For her part, Faustina Casillas acknowledges that the *cato* restriction is not altogether welcome, but has the virtue of putting all *cocalero* families on a similar footing. 'Before, some *cocaleros* had much bigger plots of land [devoted to coca],' she says; 'now those who grow more run the risk of losing their *cato*.'

The restrictions on coca production tend to apply more to the Chapare than to the Yungas, where eradication was always more difficult to implement but where also coca was sold principally on the domestic market for *acullico* and other purposes. Even if the *cato* policy has not led to much of a reduction in the number of hectares planted with coca in the Chapare, it has certainly helped stem the increase. In general, acreages in the Yungas have grown more rapidly in recent years than in the Chapare, where in 2010 there was actually a decrease recorded. Eradication efforts meanwhile have been maintained (albeit at a much lower level than in the 1990s), with the focus on reducing production of coca in areas like national parks, where it is actually forbidden. In 2011, the area eradicated increased to 10,000 hectares, almost as much as in the whole of Peru (a much bigger country) that year.

The impact of coca production on the local economy is also difficult to assess. Prices paid for Bolivian coca – whether in official markets or clandestine ones – have increased somewhat in recent years. A big increase was a direct impact of the 'zero coca' programme (from US$1.2 per kilogram in 1995 to US$5.7 in 2000), but they did not return to that level once eradication eased. Prices declined somewhat between 2004 and 2007, but have increased again since then, partly reflecting a sharp decrease in plantings in Colombia. According to UNODC, the average price for Chapare coca in 2010 was US$5.8 per kilogram. The UN estimates that coca production in 2010 was worth around US$310 million, or 1.7 per cent of GDP.

If data on coca cultivation is problematic, it is even more so for cocaine production in Bolivia. The UNODC, as well as others, are of the opinion that cocaine manufacture is on the increase, in large part because the squeeze applied in recent years in Colombia has forced Colombian drug makers and traffickers southwards into Peru and Bolivia. The UNODC says that it has evidence that, as a consequence, the levels of efficiency of cocaine production have increased; it now takes less coca to produce a given amount of cocaine. Estimates of the amounts of dried coca leaves available for cocaine production rose substantially in both countries between 2005 and 2010 – in Peru from 97,000 mt to 120,500 mt and in Bolivia from 28,200 mt to 40,200 mt – though this is not proof of their being used to this end. Estimates of pure cocaine manufacture also rose, in Bolivia's case from 80 mt to 113 mt between 2005 and 2008. Such figures, it needs to be stressed, are little more than guesstimates. Unsurprisingly, *cocaleros* are coy when it comes to commenting on the activities of illicit buyers and cocaine interests. 'Of course there are some people about who are involved in drug trafficking,' says Israel Barrenechea at Radio Kawsachun Coca, 'but it's not altogether obvious who they are.' New areas of production are often reported: in highland communities, national parks and intermediate-level towns.

Policy in Bolivia meanwhile has shifted from coca eradication to more effective repression of cocaine manufacture and trafficking. The figures made available by the Bolivian authorities suggest that these efforts have borne some fruit. Reported seizures of cocaine base, for example, rose from 12 mt in 2006 to 25.7 mt in 2010, an increase of 17 per cent per annum. The figures for pure cocaine seizures rose from 1.3 mt to 3.4 mt over the same period. Similarly, the reported destruction of cocaine manufacturing facilities, including maceration pits, was also up substantially over this period. In October 2012, the government led a clampdown on cocaine paste manufacture in both Yapacaní (in Santa Cruz) and in Challapata in the Altiplano. As a result, prices of coca fell sharply and producers were unable to find alternative buyers.

Relatively little of Bolivia's production now goes to the United States, and western Europe has emerged as the main destination. Much of it is shipped through Brazil. Bolivia is also a trans-shipment route for cocaine originating in Peru and headed for the European market. In 2011, Bolivia signed an agreement with Brazil to tighten up controls on cocaine flows through (or to) Brazil.

Living conditions in the Chapare

The ease-up in the eradication of coca, coupled with improved prices for the leaf, seems have led to a significant improvement in living standards for most people in the Chapare. People talked of having incomes of 1,000–2,000 bolivianos (US$145–290) per month. According to Segundina Orellana, from Mariscal Sucre B, living conditions were extremely tough during the period of 'zero coca'. 'We had only just enough to survive,' she says; 'thanks to coca, we have been able to improve the family economy.' While admitting that smaller plots of coca have had an impact on living standards, Faustina Casillas says that this has been offset by higher prices in recent years. Also, she points out that coca is by no means the only crop in the Chapare, and that almost all families grow rice, cassava (yuca) and maize, as well as citrus fruits and pineapple. 'The problem is that there isn't much of a market for these, and we need help from the government to generate other forms of production,' she says. For his part, José Luis Colque at Radio Kawsachun Coca sees that people have benefited materially in the last few years, spending the money not just on cars and suchlike, but also on improving their homes. The pace of urbanization is notable in the Chapare, with increasing numbers actually living in towns. Places like Shinahota and Chimoré, previously makeshift shanty towns, have grown rapidly, sporting new buildings made of brick and concrete. Colque notes that 'ten years ago most people lived in wooden shacks, but today you can see plenty of buildings of three or even four storeys'. At the same time, there have been improvements in health and education provision in the area, until recently largely absent outside the main urban centres.

But the most important change in the minds of most of those we interviewed was not so much improvements in material living standards as the climate of peace and tranquillity that came about with the ending of militarization and forced eradication. Faustina Casillas, born and brought up some seventy-five kilometres from Villa Tunari and the daughter of a *dirigente*, recalls how the climate of physical insecurity compounded the economic problems caused by 'zero coca'. 'We were in permanent struggle under a succession of governments,' she says; 'we lived in a state of total mayhem.' In the words of Elizabeth Yucra from the Federación Tupaj Katari, 'previously we were constantly persecuted [...] we suffered times of great fear'. The key to these advances – both in incomes and the general environment – was attributed by our interviewees to the achievement of organizational unity. Faustina says, 'here we are organized, but this is not the case everywhere [...] we have to consolidate the unity among us, to be a single voice at the national level'.

Another notable change in the Chapare, as elsewhere in Bolivia, is the achievement of rights among those who previously had none. Nowhere is this more evident than among women. 'The constitution guarantees women's rights,' says Elizabeth Yucra; 'we have achieved equality of gender and as women we now occupy positions in public life.' The role of women within the social movements of the Chapare was clear to us from the meeting we attended at Lauca Ñ. Women were much in evidence both in leadership roles and as delegates to the meeting, although in our interview with Faustina Casillas she was adamant that there was still a long way to go in achieving gender equality.

As elsewhere, the introduction of targeted subsidies has benefited women, as it has the elderly. According to Segundina Orellana, 'the Renta Dignidad has helped augment family incomes, as well as provide a degree of independence for those over sixty [...] It has brought a lot of benefits,' she says. However, not all people eligible actually receive the Renta Dignidad. Raquel Chipana, who works on a project in Chimoré supported by HelpAge International, argues that the Renta Dignidad and social security provision for the elderly represent important advances. The problem, she notes, is how to translate these into practice: the 30 per cent discount for older people on public transport is widely ignored, for instance. 'Many people have no idea of their rights,' she claims, while lots of older people lack the documentation needed to claim benefits. 'Most of the older people are migrants [from the Altiplano], and as such lack papers like birth certificates,' she says. One of the more practical methods to overcome this problem is to 'get yourself baptized anew' and to use a certificate of baptism to access benefits.

Chipana is far from complacent about the problems facing the elderly in the Chapare in spite of the benefits now available. She argues that most people live in conditions of poverty and often suffer mistreatment, 'working like peons on the family *chacra* [agricultural plot]'. Working conditions are also far from easy for the average *cocalero*, who can expect to labour for as much as twelve hours a day. Also, material benefits are not an unmixed blessing, according to José Luis Colque. He says that 'one of the real problems in the area is the decay of the family unit [...] there is a rising degree of materialism that undermines social solidarity'.

Notwithstanding such problems, there is clearly a strong sense of loyalty to both Evo and the MAS government in the Chapare. As Faustina Casillas put it, 'We feel great pride to have a president who came from here [...], one who started as a union leader.' This effusive support for Morales is reciprocated by the president himself, who maintains strong links with his own base, travelling to the region frequently and appearing as 'one of the people'. By not relinquishing his position as president of the Federación del Trópico when elected president (or since), Morales has deliberately maintained the organic link with his most fervent supporters. As Elizabeth Yucra sees it, 'thanks to our struggle, our president is now president of Bolivia [...] thanks to this we have grown in organizational strength'. People in the Chapare feel they have contributed to change in the country and are proud to see some of the results; those we spoke to were well informed and their thinking went far beyond preoccupation solely with their own problems.

Organization and living standards in the Yungas

As we have seen, the Yungas has a rather different history from the Chapare. Coca growing goes back to earliest times, well before the Spanish invasion. It is cultivated on terraced hillsides, not on flat plantations. The leaf is different to that of the Chapare, and is more sought after for *acullico*. A greater proportion of coca leaves therefore is consumed nationally, and proportionately less goes into the manufacture of cocaine. Partly because of the hilly geography of the region, and partly because of the degree of community organization, eradication has never been pursued with the same ferocity as was the case in the Chapare. The business of coca growing in the Yungas has tended to be more regulated than that in the Chapare. Most coca is sold through the Villa Fatima market in La Paz, and to be able to sell coca there, producers must be able to show their official producer carnet. 'To get your carnet, you first need to have the backing of your local *sindicato*,' says Alison Spedding, a British-born academic who has spent years living with and studying the *cocaleros* of the South Yungas province.

As in the Chapare, the Yungas is organizationally dominated by the *sindicato agrario*, which has a strongly entrenched presence throughout society in the region. Each community belongs to a *subcentral* or to a *central*, where the number of communities exceeds twelve. These then belong to a federation at the level of the province, although in some cases there are areas within provinces that have federations of their own. As of the mid-1990s, there appears to have been an overall strengthening of the union structure, particularly at the intermediate level, i.e. at the level of the *central* or *sub-central*. According to Spedding, meetings take place more regularly and levels of participation within them are much higher than before. 'Previously they [the union branches] hardly ever met up,' she says; 'now they meet regularly every month, and sometimes more often than that.' This greater level of activity places pressure on provincial and departmental leaderships to adhere to voices from below.

The threat of coca eradication has been a stimulus to organization. Dionicio Núñez, a vice-minister for coca in Evo Morales's second administration, who was previously a coca union leader from La Asunta, recalls how, between 2000 and 2003, the government sought to deploy troops to the Yungas. 'This led to a general mobilization that lasted ten days,' he says; 'we held the military officers hostage in the barracks in Chulumani [...] this forced the government to send ministers to negotiate with us.' It was in this context, amid *bloqueos* and marches, that the MAS built up electoral support. According to Núñez, the MAS won by a landslide in the Yungas in the 2002 presidential elections, let alone those of 2005. But since then, political divisions have emerged, especially since 2010. Núñez recalls how in that year the government made the tactical blunder during the municipal election campaign of talking about the need for 'rationalizing' coca. This was widely taken as a euphemism for introducing policies of crop eradication. Consequently, the MAS lost control over a number of municipalities. Support for the party is therefore not unconditional.

Official policy, at least since 2008, has been to differentiate between the so-called '*cordón tradicional*', areas where coca has been grown for generations, and new areas, where coca growing has increased substantially in recent years. These include some areas that are national parks. In such areas, eradication teams have sought forcibly to reduce coca acreages. The Morales government, despite protestations of sovereignty, has sought to take steps to reduce the amounts of coca grown, or at least to stem its growth into new geographical areas. The system of social control, exercised through the *sindicato*, is somewhat similar to that of the Chapare, though the *cato* (where it has been accepted) is somewhat larger in the Yungas, measuring 2,500 square metres, or 50 metres by 50 metres. In most parts of the Yungas, however, no limit has so far been imposed because, in Spedding's view, it would lead to an insurrection.

Meanwhile, the relationship between the *sindicato* and the MAS is a sensitive one. For some, at least, there is a danger of *sindicatos* being co-opted into instruments to control coca growing. Spedding points to the historical analogy of the MNR's control over the peasant movement in the 1950s, when unions were effectively manipulated from above. For his part, Núñez comments how difficult it has become to be in government and to maintain ties with the grass roots. 'They call us *oficialistas*, often a dirty word,' he says. 'But we *are oficialistas*,' he adds. 'People need to realize it is not the same *oficialismo* as before.'

As in the Chapare, living standards have certainly improved in the Yungas. The number of cars in the region is one indicator, as is the proliferation of brick-built homes, televisions and the use of other consumer durables of one kind or another. Dionicio Núñez recalls how in La Asunta, a decade ago, hardly anyone had their own car, and that there were only two or three buses in the town. 'Now almost everyone has a car,' he says. In the South Yungas, around Asunta, Spedding sees the same phenomenon. 'Previously people had to walk from one place to another – not now,' she says, citing the fact that those who do not own cars travel around the place in radio taxis. She also points to the fact that diseases caused or exacerbated by malnutrition or contaminated water supplies are things of the past. In part, this improvement reflects the extension of public services in an area where these were largely lacking only a few years ago. But it also reflects the rise in people's income, derived largely from the good prices they are receiving for increased coca production. The *bonos*, the subsidized payments paid by the state to specific groups such as the elderly, nursing mothers and schoolchildren, have a symbolic value for people, but they do not compare with the income that can be derived from growing coca, or even just picking it. Women picking coca can earn 80–100 bolivianos a day. Spedding reports on how conditions for labourers have improved. 'You have to ship them in in microbuses, and you can't get away with giving them the cheapest *refresco* to drink; they want Coca-Cola,' she says.

Conclusions

Coca is an important source of income for a substantial sector of the Bolivian population. It is also a crop that has deep cultural and religious significance. Although Bolivia is an important producer of cocaine for the world market, the Morales government has taken steps both to curtail coca production and to clamp down on cocaine output. The policies of social control have been an important factor in ensuring that Bolivian coca acreages have not increased dramatically in recent years, despite market encouragement to grow more coca because of the relatively high prices available. They appear to have been more successful – and certainly more socially acceptable – than forcible eradication of the sort applied in the 1990s. The attempt to suppress cocaine production is far more problematic, as shifting patterns in global cocaine output (the balloon effect) make Bolivia more attractive than Colombia as a place to manufacture cocaine. A by-product of the one *cato* per family policy appears to have been to engender greater equality among coca-producing families.

The *cocaleros* of the Chapare, as well as those of the Yungas, represent a core constituency for Morales and the MAS. In the Chapare, people we spoke to referred to Evo as their '*líder indiscutible*' (unquestionable leader). They saw themselves and their parents before them as key agents in the 'process of change' and as exercising influence over the course of government policy. As such, they showed a degree of political consciousness that went far beyond simple defence of their own interests. They also showed a keen awareness of the importance of social organization (which they saw as helping them defeat the zero coca policy) and participation. The *ampliado* we witnessed at Lauca Ñ revealed an important degree of grassroots participation in decision-making. The increased role of women within that social organization was striking. But in spite of their support for Morales, it was by no means always the case that the *cocaleros* would blithely accept policies enacted from above, particularly when these threatened their interests and undercut their incomes.

That people felt they had benefited overall from the policies of the last few years was without doubt. The ending of the militarization of the 'war on drugs' had given *cocaleros* in the Chapare the ability to rebuild their economy and society. There were clear signs, both in the Chapare and the Yungas, that living standards had increased. While this may have been due primarily to the buoyancy of the coca economy, it was also the result of deliberate policy. As elsewhere, poor families felt they had benefited from targeted income supplements. There was also wide recognition of the benefits received from other areas of policy, such as improved health and educational provision. Most of those we spoke to attributed the advances made to the importance of organizational unity. But whether solidarity will survive patterns of urbanization and improved living standards, as José Luis Colque surmised, will only become clearer over the longer run. Collective action presupposes some sort of adversary, and the let-up in repression among the *cocaleros* may, if sustained, lead to less by way of social control. However, our interviews suggested that the institutions of the coca-producing areas, particularly the *sindicato*, remain very strong, with little scope for individual dissidence. The political culture of the *cocaleros* and their families will probably not change rapidly in spite of growing individualism in the wider society.

6 | OF GAS, RENTS AND INDIGENOUS MOVEMENTS OF THE CHACO

The town of Villamontes bears the signs of new-found wealth. One of the gas capitals of the Bolivian Chaco, its streets are paved in concrete, laid out in wide boulevards with state-of-the-art street lighting and traffic management systems. It has been the beneficiary of copious spending on infrastructure projects generally, and boasts a brand-new market, a hospital and modern sporting facilities. A spanking-new bridge over the River Pilcomayo, 502 metres in length, means that traffic heading north to Santa Cruz or south to the Argentine border no longer has to drive across the old railway bridge, previously the only connection on this important north–south route. But cross the bridge and you enter a different world. Capirandita, some four kilometres south of Villamontes and down a rutted track off a new road that eventually leads to Paraguay, is where the Organization of Captains of the Weenhayek (Orcaweta) have their headquarters.

This settlement of the Weenhayek, one of three main ethnic groups of the Gran Chaco in Tarija department, reveals the other side of the development coin. The roads are unpaved, the houses rudimentary and the infrastructure primitive. Pigs roll in the dust, goats shelter from the burning sun under the spiny scrub, and kids play in the street. We went to meet Moisés Sapirenda, leader (*capitán grande*) of the Weenhayek, who pointed ruefully to the development of Villamontes across the other side of the river. 'Look at the bridge they have built, look at the paved streets' – and he adds (perhaps with a touch of exaggeration), 'it's just like Miami'. The Weenhayek believe they have not received their fair share of the development boom that the discovery of gas has brought to Tarija. Indeed, a good deal of it is under their land. 'The gas is under our feet and the pipelines cross our backyard,' Moisés says.

The discovery of major gas reserves in Tarija in the 1990s and the construction of pipelines leading to Argentina and Brazil have had a huge impact on the Bolivian economy in recent years. Gas production increased from an average of 19.6 million cubic metres per day (cm/d) in 2001 to an announced 51.9 million cm/d in 2012. In the first half of 2012, gas exports (mainly to Brazil) accounted for a fraction under half of total export earnings. And, as of 2006, when the Morales government renationalized the hydrocarbons industry and raised the taxes payable by oil and gas companies, gas revenues have become the mainstay of public finances and the key to poverty alleviation. Bolivia's chronic fiscal deficit up until 2006 turned into a substantial surplus thereafter. And the revenues gained from gas exports provided the key prop to the growth in Bolivia's international reserves. On a per capita basis, these were among the highest anywhere in Latin America in 2011. The recovery of the Bolivian economy from the doldrums of the late 1990s and early 2000s owes much to the production of gas in Tarija.

Yet, as we shall see, the benefits for the people of Tarija, particularly the indigenous from whose lands much of the gas is extracted, have been far from equally shared. Within Tarija, some of the largest gas fields – like the Margarita mega-field – lie within legally recognized indigenous regions (Tierras Comunitarias de Orígen – TCOs) that enjoy a degree of autonomy. And there is an uncanny correlation elsewhere too between areas with oil and gas potential and those that have been designated indigenous regions and national parks. The area with the greatest hydrocarbons potential stretches in an arc parallel to the eastern edge of the Andes from northern Argentina right through Bolivia up to the Camisea gas fields in Peru and beyond. Many of the contracts with oil and gas companies, whether active or not, are on land that has been formally designated as TCOs (or TIOCs as they are now called).

Two worlds superimposed

The development of Bolivia's hydrocarbons potential goes back to the 1920s. Until the industry was nationalized in 1937, the main operator in Bolivia was the US company Standard Oil of New Jersey. One of the factors giving rise to the devastating war in the Chaco between 1932 and 1935 between Bolivia and Paraguay was the belief that the region was a major source of oil wealth. The main company involved in Paraguay at the time was British-owned Royal Dutch Shell. The Chaco War saw huge loss of life on both sides, not least among indigenous people from the highlands, drafted into the army. As it turned out, though Bolivia lost a large swathe of territory, it – and not Paraguay – retained control over the areas where oil and gas were subsequently to be found. The first nationalization in 1937 (Bolivia is one of the very few countries to nationalize its hydrocarbons industry three times) and the creation of Yacimientos Petrolíferos Fiscales Bolivianos (YPFB) failed to lead to new reserves. In the 1950s a deal was struck with Gulf Oil to develop the industry, resulting in significant new discoveries. In 1969, Bolivian Gulf Oil was nationalized, with YPFB taking over its assets.

By the 1990s, however, under the government of Gonzalo Sánchez de Lozada, YPFB was again part privatized under the modality of 'capitalization'. Foreign companies were offered attractive fiscal and other inducements to invest in Bolivia, and an important gas pipeline linking Bolivia with the urban metropolis of São Paulo was constructed. Although YPFB claims it had identified important new gas reserves in Bolivia prior to capitalization, it was the foreign companies which subsequently took the credit for these. They included Petrobras (Brazil), Repsol (Spain), Total (France) and British Gas (UK). Of the gas fields discovered, three of the biggest – San Antonio, San Alberto and Margarita – are all located in the department of Tarija. Sophisticated drilling techniques plus access to markets made this possible. As a consequence of a new hydrocarbons law, passed in 2005 (before Morales came to power), the relationship between the state and the private sector once again shifted. Contracts with foreign firms were changed in 2006 from joint ventures to service contracts, YPFB assuming a more central role in the industry. At the same time, the tax regime was changed, forcing these companies to pay substantially more in royalties (on production) and in direct taxation (IDH) on their operating profits.

The development of indigenous organization in the lowlands of Bolivia is of more recent date than that of the hydrocarbons industry, though the two have affected one another in a variety of ways. The 1990s saw the growth of the Confederación de Pueblos Indígenas de Bolivia (Cidob), among whose founding members was the Chaco-based Asamblea del Pueblo Guaraní (APG), founded in 1987. Though the Guaraníes, the main ethnic grouping in the Chaco region, had violently opposed the inroads made by outsiders during both the colonial and republican periods, they were crushed militarily at the end of the nineteenth century. With the extension of the hacienda system in the Chaco, particularly livestock rearing, the Guaraní became servile labour on massive landed estates. The agrarian reform of 1953 did not recognize the existence of ethnic groups like the Guaraní, the Weenhayek and the Tapieté. It also had a perverse effect on lowland indigenous peoples like the Guaraní by encouraging the development of agro-exporting industries and the settlement of highland indigenous people in the east. It proved fairly easy for newcomers to exploit the splits and divisions within people like the Guaraní. In the words of Eufronio Toro, then director of CIPCA (a rural promotion agency) in Camiri, 'it was state policy to deprive them [the Guaraní] of their lands'.

It was only in the 1990s that state policy towards lowland indigenous peoples in the east began to change. In part, this was due to the organization and mobilization of lowland indigenous groups, especially the landmark march organized by the Cidob from Trinidad to La Paz in 1990. The foundation of the APG and the activities of institutions like CIPCA also highlighted the acute problems of semi-slavery (*servidumbre*) and social deprivation among the Guaraní. In the mid-1980s, an influential study was undertaken which showed that 30 per cent of Guaraní families had less than a half-hectare of land, and suggested that the Guaraní were heading for extinction. The issue of landownership and distribution in the Chaco thus gained some salience. It was the Sánchez de Lozada government in the 1990s which took an important initiative in this respect with the passage in 1996 of the INRA Law. The new legislation introduced the concept of the indigenous TCO, and set out a programme to resolve landownership issues (*saneamiento*) and to give indigenous peoples and campesinos title to the land. This led to the establishment of a number of TCOs in the Chaco and farther north in Santa Cruz and the Beni, also recognizing the existence of third-party settlements (privately owned farms) within them. This has often led to big problems for the TCOs.

In the Chaco, basically the eastern parts of Tarija and Chuquisaca and the southern part of Santa Cruz department, Guaraní peoples took advantage of these new opportunities. They were keen to take part in processes of *saneamiento*, though implementation of the INRA Law encountered serious obstacles – not least opposition from the region's large landowners. Previously, the Guaraní had tried to acquire their own land, often putting down money to do so. However, since the promulgation of the INRA Law, local indigenous peoples have become increasingly well organized and self-assertive, particularly with respect to land and territory. In the view of Alejandrina Avenante, a Guaraní from a community just north of Villamontes, the establishment of defendable land rights forms the basis for all other social, economic and political demands. 'You need ownership [of land] to be able to make other demands,' she says, referring to the difficulties of complaining about oil spills on their land.

It was almost inevitable, then, that increased consciousness of rights on the part of indigenous peoples would clash with the aspirations of oil and gas companies. The relationship between the two, particularly in the 1990s, became one of increased confrontation over the procedures to be used to allow hydrocarbons companies to explore for and exploit oil and gas reserves in indigenous areas. The hydrocarbons law, passed by Sánchez de Lozada in 1996, stipulated that the relationship between local populations and hydrocarbons companies was a relationship between private entities, and therefore outside the purview of the state, an argument also used more recently. This was in spite of Bolivia having subscribed in 1991 to the International Labour Organization's 1989 Convention 169 on the responsibility of the state to ensure prior consultation with indigenous peoples where extractive industries operate on their land.

In most cases where companies sought to engage with local people and negotiate their presence, the tactics used sought to avoid expensive outcomes for the former. Often corporate social responsibility (CSR) was limited to such activities as providing pencils and notebooks for children, desks for local schools or building sporting facilities in indigenous communities. Such dealings were conducted on an individual basis with communities, not with ethnic groupings or their leaders. CSR was later directed towards local projects, sometimes with municipalities. But to the Guaraní, concessions made by companies to local needs were simply a response to local organization and the demands made. According to Avenante, 'We have to go in to make demands of them; otherwise they take no notice [...] the problem is that we have not known how to make demands.' She goes on to say that 'what they give us is just something to keep us quiet'. The issue of prior consultation as a right is not something that oil and gas companies – at least until recent times – have been prepared to concede willingly. Issues of compensation for social or environmental damage caused by extractive industries have been made only under duress. And the idea that indigenous peoples might share in the profits made from the resources extracted 'from under our feet' is a notion even less enthusiastically embraced by the companies involved.

The impact of gas on Tarija

With around 80 per cent of Bolivia's gas reserves and a correspondingly high proportion of its production, the development of the industry has had a major impact on the local economy in Tarija, on society and on local politics. According to figures cited by Roberto Ruiz, the secretary-general of the departmental government (*gobernación*) in Tarija, the amount of money available has increased enormously. The annual budget between 2001 and 2004 averaged 500 million bolivianos. In the period between 2005 and 2010, it averaged 2.2 billion bolivianos. In 2011, the budget was 3.17 billion, and in 2012 it was expected to reach 3.8 billion. As well as a result of increased prices for gas sold to Brazil and Argentina, much of this increase was attributable to Tarija's share in royalties (distributed also to gas-producing municipalities) and its share in the overall IDH tax on hydrocarbons profits (shared with the other eight departments), as well as revenues from local taxes. Again, according to Ruiz, the royalties paid to Tarija in the twenty years between 1974 and 1994 totalled US$140 million, an average of US$7 million a year. In 2012, by contrast, the royalties paid were expected to be of the order of US$500 million.

This bonanza has led to serious problems in spending the money available. Again, according to Ruiz, the amount of the budget that the *gobernación* was unable to spend was 350 million bolivianos in 2009 (around US$50 million), 840 million in 2010 and 940 million in 2011. The problem of spending has been made worse, he says, by the fact that the strict anti-corruption legislation introduced by the Morales administration at the national level created disincentives for officials to spend money unless the paperwork is 100 per cent correct: 'If everything is not in perfect order, they prefer to do nothing,' he says. Money tends to be used on infrastructure projects, rather than longer-term productive ones.

According to Carlos Vacaflores at JAINA, a local research centre, there has been highly wasteful public spending in recent years on projects of doubtful longer-term utility, and a fierce dispute for resources between different groups. Under the governorship of Mario Cossío, a strident opponent of the Morales administration, there was a sharp increase in public spending, which led to 'poor investments and increased corruption', in the opinion of Miguel Castro, another local analyst. Cossío's decision to go into self-imposed exile in 2010 amid charges of corruption and graft has not led to much of an improvement. The government of Lino Condori, an interim governor from the MAS, does not seem to have improved matters noticeably. 'The new administration isn't up to the challenges it faces,' says Castro.

Historically, the department of Tarija has been highly centralized in the capital city, situated in a fertile inter-Andean valley at around 2,500 metres above sea level towards the west of the department. The city and surrounding area account for a large proportion of the total population, with a considerable influx of migration from highland Bolivia, particularly from neighbouring Potosí and Chuquisaca over recent years. The geography of the department, and particularly a series of rugged mountain ranges going north to south, has separated the capital from the Chaco region, where the gas reserves are concentrated. Towns of the Chaco like Yacuiba and Villamontes were small by comparison with Tarija, and cut off in terms of land communications. Even today, many prefer to travel to the Chaco through Argentina rather than opt for the twisting mountainous road through Entre Ríos, the capital of O'Connor province. The final range going east, the jagged Aguaragüe sierra, gives way to the flat Chaco lowlands, spreading out towards Paraguay. The Chaco is therefore more accessible from Santa Cruz to the north than it is from Tarija city.

The distribution of gas rents has changed the balance between Tarija city and the Chaco, although indigenous groupings in the latter remain at the margins. Today, three municipalities in the Chaco – Yacuiba, Villamontes and Caraparí – share 45 per cent of the total departmental royalties, although between them they constitute less than 30 per cent of the population. Of these, Caraparí has only around 10,000 inhabitants. Reportedly it has the highest per capita income of any municipality in Latin America. These municipalities face even more serious problems in spending the available money. 'How many aqueducts are you able to build?' asks Eufronio Toro at CIPCA in Camiri. Carlos Vacaflores says that municipal finance at Caraparí is something out of Macondo (alluding to Gabriel García Márquez's famous novel *A Hundred Years of Solitude*), with the purchase of a helicopter forming part of the development plan. In his opinion, these three municipalities constitute the 'fiction of a region'. The 2009 constitution opens the way to the creation of regional autonomies within departments: the Gran Chaco is the only 'region' currently to exist.

Competition for resources within Tarija, coupled with changes in the nature of political power both within the department and nationally, has led to significant changes in local politics. One of the most significant has been the declining influence of the old elite families that have dominated the scene since well before the 1952 revolution but which survived intact through their ties with the MNR. Cossío's exit also seems to have led to a decline of previously influential institutions like the Civic Committee, in which the old elite was well represented. In the past, employment in state administrations provided a ladder to improvement and was largely dominated by local middle-class families. In place of this elite, new actors have come to the fore and with them a struggle for control over the department's burgeoning finances. The fact that, as of 2012, the president of the departmental assembly was an indigenous leader (Justino Zambrana from the Itika Guasu) and the governor of the department (Lino Condori) a peasant leader from the poorest province, Yunchará, is indicative of this change. Migration into Tarija from other parts of Bolivia has also had an important bearing on the reshaping of *tarijeño* society.

Among the protagonists of change has been the peasantry, which accounts for about 30 per cent of the population. The peasant federation, the Federación Sindical Única de Comunidades Campesinas de Tarija, was established in 1982 and has seen a considerable growth in its membership and organizational capacities in recent years. The peasant population has increased with persistent immigration from other parts of country, especially from Potosí, Sucre and La Paz. The peasants have demanded greater political representation. A consequence of increased peasant pressure has been the Prosol programme, instated by Cossío (amid other spending plans such as a popular health insurance scheme) but continued and expanded under his successor. Prosol originally involved an annual grant of 2,500 bolivianos to peasant families, an amount subsequently increased to 4,500 bolivianos. Rather than just being used individually, much of this money has been channelled into strengthening communal productive capacities through, for example, the purchase of agricultural machinery or the building of small irrigation schemes. By 2012, some 6,000 hectares of small-scale properties had been irrigated since the scheme began in 2008. Spending on Prosol rose from 43 million bolivianos in 2010 to 140 million in 2011. In the view of Carlos Vacaflores, it has successfully managed to avert the worst dangers of political clientelism in the distribution of resources. 'I think it will be difficult to reverse,' he says. It also tends to reinforce investment in rural areas and strengthen collective structures.

Other social groups have found it harder to make their mark in regional politics. They include formerly militant groups such as the unemployed and the homeless, which became increasingly vocal from the 1990s. However, since the electoral victory of the MAS in 2005, these have tended to fracture and become more diffuse. According to Ciro Rosado, himself a MAS militant, this had a good deal to do with the personal ambitions of those involved and the opportunities available to them to take positions of influence under the new government. The availability of gas-derived funds has done little to promote successful industrial projects in the department and thus provide jobs for the long term; rather, money has tended to be invested in *obras* of doubtful productive use. Of various industrial projects proposed, including factories to produce glass, cement, vegetable oil, sugar and paper, only the cement and sugar factories are working. In Rosado's opinion there is a 'severe lack of industrial management capacity' at the local level. 'We're not even able to produce nails in Bolivia,' he laments.

Indigenous organizations are also increasingly making their mark on local politics, even though they represent only a small part of the department's population. This is, in part, due to advances in their organizational capacities. These have come partly from their conflicts with gas companies. But they are also a consequence of the rights conceded to indigenous communities by the 2009 constitution. They have become empowered, whereas previously they had little or no voice in departmental politics. There are three seats in the regional assembly (out of thirty) reserved for the three main ethnic groups in the department, the Itika Guasu, the Weenhayek and the Tapieté. Of these the latter are only a small grouping, much smaller than the other two. The appointment of Zambrana of the Itika Guasu as president of the departmental assembly was a consequence of his entering into an alliance with the more numerous conservative group, thus displacing the MAS from control in 2011. But the fact that he's there at all is significant. 'It's impressive that Justino is where he is,' says Miguel Castro. For his part, Zambrana is intent on increasing the political power exercised by indigenous groups. 'We need to take power in Tarija,' he says, 'we need to have twenty seats [not three].' As of mid-2012, indigenous communities were demanding a much larger slice of the local fiscal cake as part of their demands for administrative autonomy: 15 per cent of the departmental royalties from gas. If TCOs (or TIOCs) are to function autonomously, they need to secure their own funding, and this has led to demands, for example, that they should receive part of the gas royalty directly of right.

Experiences of indigenous advance

As we have seen, relations between indigenous groups and the hydrocarbons companies operating on their territories have undergone an abrupt change, particularly since the late 1990s, when exploratory activity, extraction of gas and the building of pipelines all increased; indigenous groups became aware that they enjoyed considerable leverage in striving for a better deal from the gas lying beneath their feet.

The first experiences of these sorts of advance dated from the late 1990s. The construction of the gas pipeline from Santa Cruz to São Paulo involved crossing lands belonging to indigenous groups in the Chuiquitanía in Santa Cruz department. The pipeline was financed by, among others, the World Bank. The Bank's guidelines included the requirement that projects adhere to the ILO Convention 169 on prior consultation. No such consultation took place in this instance, enabling compensation eventually being agreed for a sum of US$2.3 million to the Chiquitanos. Guaraní people also managed to gain compensation, in some instances for failure to consult them over pipelines traversing their territories.

Three instances of indigenous groups in the area responding to expanded hydrocarbons operations in their territories merit particular mention; each is rather different in its nature and outcomes.

The first of these involved the Tentayape, a small indigenous group whose TCO lands straddle the municipalities of Muyupampa and Huacareta in the *chuquisaqueño* Chaco. Their lands (10,000 hectares, so not that large) are overlapped by two concessions, Caipipendi South and Central, both awarded to a consortium involving Repsol, British Gas (BG) and Pan American Energy. In this instance, the Tentayape declared in 1997/98 that they had no interest in having gas exploration on their lands and turned down all offers of community development assistance from the gas consortium. They also rejected incursions on their lands from the ministries of health and education, churches and NGOs. In view of this stand-off, the consortium found itself obliged to withdraw from the territory of the Tentayape, a decision hailed by other indigenous groups and NGOs working to defend indigenous rights. Though emblematic, this stand-off led to conditions of life in the Tentayape TCO being somewhat romanticized by outsiders.

The second case involved the Weenhayek, whose lands spread out in an arc along the western bank of the Pilcomayo river from

Villamontes southwards to the Argentine frontier. Their TCO dates from 1992, although it is not an integrated unit inasmuch as there are other farmers living legally within their TCO, which has itself been only partially *saneado*. The Weenhayek, grouped in nearly sixty communities, were traditionally hunter-gatherers. In the last few decades, though, they have come to live primarily off the plentiful fish to be found in the Pilcomayo. Their lands include four separate contract areas owned and operated by BG Bolivia. The whole Weenhayek TCO overlaps with land in which gas has been discovered. The Weenhayek are less integrated into wider society than the Guaraní, and in recent years have suffered great hardship as a result of the collapse of fishing in the Pilcomayo due to sedimentation downstream in Paraguay and Argentina. 'The Pilcomayo used to be full of fish,' says Moisés Sapirenda, the Weenhayek's *capitán grande* in Capirandita; 'you could get five thousand fish in twenty-four hours [...] now there is virtually nothing.'

The conflicts between the Weenhayek and BG Bolivia began to develop before 2000. Faced with growing militancy among the locals, including roadblocks to prevent equipment being shipped in, BG Bolivia decided to negotiate with rather than oppose the Weenhayek. They initially agreed to pay them an annual amount of US$70,000 for twenty years, since raised to US$150,000 owing to the increase in the number of wells drilled. There is some doubt, however, as to the exact size of the funds paid since the Weenhayek are not forthcoming about the money they receive from the companies. The funds are administered fairly secretively by the assemblies of leaders of the Weenhayek, and this has itself given rise to some distrust and weakening of their organization. Initially the funds were to go to the four communities most affected, but following pressure from Cidob a sharing formula was agreed by which the bulk of the funds would flow to these communities, and the rest to the others. According to Sapirenda, the amount paid is 'not enough', but he says that relations with both BG Bolivia and Transierra (which has pipelines crossing Weenhayek land) are 'quite good'. However, others are critical of the ways in which the funds have been used, and argue that they have favoured the leaders rather than the grass roots. 'There have been big changes among the Weenhayek,' says Rolando Quiroga, who works in Villamontes on a pilot project on communal justice for the justice ministry, 'including the emergence of younger leaders with an education.' Traditionally, communities have been led by their elders, but these were largely illiterate and unable to conduct negotiations with outsiders from the hydrocarbons companies.

The third and possibly most significant instance of negotiation between indigenous groups and the gas companies has been the Itika Guasu. They occupy part of the mountainous terrain between Entre Ríos and Villamontes. Their TCO, which covers a large proportion of the municipality of Entre Ríos, includes most of a large area awarded to Repsol. This includes the Margarita field and Caipipendi South (blocks A, B and C), one of the so-called mega-fields which supplies Argentina with gas. Their TCO also includes the smaller Campo Huayco contract. A small section of the Margarita field spreads into Chuquisaca to the north. There had been some minor confrontations between the Itika Guasu and gas companies in the late 1990s, but it was only with the discovery of the mega-fields after 2004 that major clashes occurred. Andrés Segundo, from the Itika Guasu and the first *tarijeño* to become president of the national APG, was closely involved in the negotiations that took place. In an interview in Entre Ríos, he explained to us the important role played by a coalition of groups, including CEADESC (an NGO based in Cochabamba), Cer-det (an NGO in Tarija with offices in Entre Ríos and Villamontes), the APG and the Itika Guasu themselves. 'We needed people to help us negotiate with the oil/gas companies [...] it worked well.' But, he added, 'you have to make a lot of noise to get anywhere'. The *bloqueos* employed by the Itika Guasu against Repsol were contingent in forcing a settlement. External pressures were also brought to bear, including intensive lobbying of Repsol in Madrid by Intermón, a member of Oxfam International.

The original demand from the Itika Guasu was that Repsol should pay them US$25 million for compensation for the use of their lands. In 2006, Repsol made a verbal agreement to pay US$13.5 million. The final settlement was US$14.8 million, with the understanding that no subsequent claims would be lodged against the company. Attempts made to sue Repsol in the European Union and in the Inter-American Court of Human Rights (ICHR) proved unsuccessful.

The US$14.8 million settlement, a private deal between Repsol and the Itika Guasu without any involvement by the state, was the largest such deal hitherto recorded in Latin America between a hydrocarbons company and an indigenous group. The deal caused considerable friction between the APG Itika Guasu and the Morales government. The money was placed in a Brazilian bank, the Banco do Brasil, and the interest payments made payable to the leadership of the Itika Guasu. These amount to some US$60,000 a month, according to a source close to the agreement who did not wish to be identified. This landmark agreement has not gone unnoticed by other groups but remained unsurpassed at the time of writing.

The impact of such amounts on a group without strong internal organization remains a matter of some debate. According to Miguel Castro, the benefits have been slight among ordinary members of the Itika Guasu. 'Ordinary people are in the same position as seven years ago,' he says, while improvements in electrification and road building within the TCO 'would probably have happened anyway'. Other observers, such as Eufronio Toro at CIPCA, respond by arguing that the amounts received by the Itika Guasu pale into insignificance when compared to the funds being received by municipal governments in the Chaco. For Andrés Segundo, the inflow of money has brought problems as well as benefits, particularly in the use of these resources and the scope for abuse on the part of community leaders. He says that his plan for each community to draw up a list of their development needs 'was not accepted' by the Itika Guasu leadership. The leaders remain aloof and several people said that they feared that the Itika Guasu were becoming cut off from the rest of society.

The Itika Guasu have also won other significant claims regarding their territory. They eventually took a claim against the departmental roads authority (SEDECA) to the constitutional tribunal in Sucre. They won their case in a verdict handed down in October 2010. The dispute had lasted four years, and related to installations built on their land. The case was particularly significant since the court ruled that there had to be prior consultation and reparation for the damages caused. The verdict, based in part on a case brought in the IACHR (*Saramaca* v. *Suriname*) creates an important precedent in Bolivian law on prior consultation.

Farther north in the department of Santa Cruz, there have also been important advances in the bid by the Guaraní to increase the political influence they wield in protecting their lands and communities. These have focused on the creation of indigenous autonomies at the municipal level. One of the most important experiences here has been in the municipality of Charagua, one of the largest in area anywhere in Bolivia. The Guaraní there have sought to win acceptance for their statutes of indigenous autonomy. At the time of writing, these were still in draft form. There had been resistance from non-indigenous people in Charagua, particularly in the town itself, as well as from cattle farmers. 'It's a struggle for power,' says Toro at CIPCA, 'but the indigenous people know they are in the majority locally.' Another municipality where statutes were under discussion was Huacaya, farther south in Chuquisaca and potentially an important area of gas production. Inasmuch as the Guaraní win power at the local level, their ability to negotiate with gas companies can only increase.

Political and economic change since 2006

The expansion of the gas industry in the Chaco region (including that of Santa Cruz and Chuquisaca, as well as Tarija) has, as we have seen, brought significant change to the region. But so too has change in power nationally. In particular, the passage of the 2009 constitution has had major implications for those living in the region, especially indigenous communities. Their legal rights have been enhanced, as has their ability to govern themselves not only in their own territories but also through the establishment of indigenous municipalities. Although the constitution took over two years to elaborate, its full implementation may take much longer, and doubts remain over the extent to which its provisions will ever be fully enacted and enforced. Still, for many we interviewed, the new constitution stood as a point of departure for the enhancement of indigenous rights. 'I see the constitution as a big step forward,' says Alejandrina Avenante, who works on Guaraní broadcasts at Radio ACLO in Tarija, 'particularly as it makes prior consultation obligatory.' Enrique Camargo, a teacher at the Guaraní university at Macharetí, sees good intentions behind the new constitution: 'the CPE is very progressive, but it's putting it into

effect that is the problem'. Moreover, he considers that participation
in the Constituent Assembly had been a hugely significant learning
process for those involved.

Closely connected with the constitutional right to prior consultation is that of land rights. The consolidation of the TCOs established
in the late 1990s has been slow to take place in this part of Bolivia;
there are still areas not yet recognized as TCOs, such as the APG
Yaku Igua and the APG Caraparí. 'The question of land remains
an issue,' says Avenante, 'and *saneamiento* is still incomplete.' The
presence of third parties in TCOs, many people of some substance,
remains a strong bone of contention in the Chaco, even though
they may officially comply with the rules governing productive use
of the land. Indigenous leaders want the government to help them
gain complete control over TCOs. But recognition of land rights has
been an important first step towards the defence of other indigenous
rights and has contributed to people's empowerment. 'This is gaining momentum,' says Camargo. 'It has been established that the
Guaraní have land rights, and consultation is becoming established,'
he adds. However, prior consultation has yet to become a standard
practice that both indigenous communities and others who want
to tap natural resources see as a necessity. 'The mechanisms of
consultation will become very important when people realize that
it works for them,' Camargo says.

The passage of the 2005 hydrocarbons law also had important
implications with respect to protecting the interests of local communities. This had twenty-two articles that dealt with questions of
indigenous rights. It also dealt with the issue of prior consultation,
as did the detailed regulations governing the application of the law,
passed in 2007. In 2005, there was a debate over whether it was prefer-
able to include the issue of prior consultation in the law, or to await
a fully fledged framework law to deal with consultation across the
board. As Adriana Soto at CEADESC (an NGO that has been involved
in many oil and gas disputes) puts it: 'indigenous people who are
hunters prefer to have a bird in the hand [the hydrocarbons law]
than one in the bush'.

In other spheres, too, there have been important changes affecting
the Guaraní. Of great importance have been the steps taken finally

to end conditions of semi-slavery (*servidumbre*), in which indigenous peoples were obliged to work for landowners without remuneration. According to Eufronio Toro, 'there are some members of the Guaraní who are still *empatronados* on private estates, but the government has shown a will to do something about this'. With Alejandro Almaraz, the vice-minister in charge of land distribution until 2010, there were clear attempts to clamp down on landowners using this practice. According to the law, such conditions are a pretext for expropriation.

Closely connected with the issues of land tenure and *servidumbre* is that of gender rights. Mariel Paz, who between 2002 and 2010 served as departmental ombudsman (*defensora del pueblo*), has studied sexual violence among Guaraní communities. What comes out of her work is that this is a consequence of deeply rooted conditioning factors, and a common denominator of sexual abuse of women is lack of land. 'Because of the lack of land, families split up, suffer extreme poverty and often end up in *servidumbre*,' she says. Historically, women are selected to become wives without having a say as to who their partner is, although Paz says that this practice is now changing. Alcoholism in communities can lead to sexual abuse by men and machismo is ingrained. 'Poverty means that sexual abuse is more open, more cruel,' she says; 'we have received testimonies of humiliation that are hard to believe.'

The extension of judicial rights in the Chaco is still fairly incipient, particularly in terms of implementing communitarian practices, but some progress is also being made. According to Rolando Quiroga, who has worked on a justice ministry project in Villamontes, the Itika Guasu have been involved in setting the frontiers between the respective jurisdictions of ordinary law and communitarian justice, in line with the Ley de Deslinde, which came into effect in 2010 (establishing the boundaries between indigenous and national legal systems). The ministry has worked on establishing integrated justice centres (*centros integrados de justicia*) in some of the larger towns of the Chaco, in the hope that these will help deal with reconciliation issues and reduce chronic congestion in the formal legal system. According to Quiroga, the Guaraní tend to be more integrated into formal state structures than the Weenhayek. The latter 'have their own systems of reconciliation', he says.

The period since 2006 has seen a significant increase in other areas of state activity, particularly in road building and education. The thirty-four communities within the Itika Guasu (thirty-two in Tarija and two in Chuquisaca) are now all connected by road, and this is seen as progress by Andrés Segundo, the former president of the APG. 'At least our children can get to school,' he says. Educational provision has improved too, with primary schools in the main communities and a secondary school at Ñaurenda, the main settlement within the TCO. 'We have received help here both from the municipality [of Entre Ríos] and the *gobernación* [in Tarija city],' he says. Among the Weenhayek, too, there have been significant improvements in educational provision. 'There are plenty of us who have received education, 150 up to completion of secondary school [...] the problem is that there's nowhere for them to continue studying,' says Moisés Sapirenda in Capirandita. The same change in education is also observed by Enrique Camargo. When asked what notable changes he had seen in recent years, he pointed both to the reconstitution of indigenous territories and to the spread of educational facilities. 'Education is a way to mobilize the defence of [indigenous] rights,' he observed.

Most of those we interviewed doubted the degree to which levels of poverty and discrimination had been substantially reduced in the indigenous communities of the Chaco. In spite of the resources made available, these had not changed ordinary people's living conditions in any major way. In Camargo's opinion, despite the changes in towns and cities, 'in the communities people still light their homes with oil lamps [*mecheros*], they carry water in buckets from far-off wells, levels of illiteracy are high, and women frequently die in pregnancy'. When asked what he thought '*vivir bien*' meant in practice, he answered, 'is it to *vivir bien* when some have all the services at their disposal as the oil company workers do, while others are drinking dirty water?' The problem of growing inequalities within indigenous communities, as well as inequalities at the level of the department as a whole, came out strongly in our interviews. 'Material living standards for most have not changed that much,' says Mariel Paz, 'and discrimination continues.' In the opinion of Miguel Castro, tackling poverty 'has been the hardest nut to crack

[...] redistribution has proved very difficult [...] it's not what we had hoped for'.

Therefore, perhaps where the greatest changes have taken place has been at the level of popular organization. As we have seen, there has been a significant increase in the powers at the disposal of indigenous communities, both with respect to the self-management of TCOs and within local politics more generally. Among the peasantry of Tarija, too, there has been significant change, perhaps more real empowerment than among indigenous peoples. The impact of programmes like Prosol, funded mainly from the gas rents, has led to an important shift in the structure of power within the department. These changes have been at the expense of traditional elites. For the middle class, Mariel Paz thinks that the tide has turned, with new people involved in state functions. Meanwhile, consciousness of social and ethnic rights has spread. Whatever the future holds for Tarija and the Chaco more generally, it will not be a return to the status quo.

Conclusions

With its copious gas resources, Tarija has become the dynamo of national development. Its role is thus somewhat similar in this respect to the mining departments of Bolivia in previous times. Owing to its importance as a source of fiscal revenues, it therefore plays a key role in any strategy of redistribution based on export rents. However, the issue of how local people participate – particularly the indigenous peoples under whose lands the gas deposits are located – has not been adequately settled. The interviews we conducted show how, even where it is carried out, prior consultation has been insufficient. Natural gas has come to dictate the terms of the relationship between the state and indigenous groups in the Chaco. Indigenous people feel that they should have a greater say over what happens in their territories and who should receive the benefits of extractive activity. The government argues that the public good is paramount.

Part of the answer may be in helping indigenous peoples, who remain economically disadvantaged, make optimum use of the lands they now possess. The new constitution points to the rights of indigenous peoples to participate in the benefits of non-renewable natural resources on their lands, but the concessions offered so far by oil and gas companies have operated on an ad hoc basis – usually in response to political pressure, not on the basis of institutional accords that carry a state guarantee. Further discussion is necessary to determine how concretely indigenous peoples can receive the benefits that the constitution offers. Similarly, development of indigenous autonomy, within TCOs and indigenous municipalities, from an economic point of view – through improved conditions locally – is also an urgent task.

A related point is the way in which indigenous peoples see their autonomies developing, particularly as regards their relationship with the wider society. With political (and economic) autonomy established locally, what role do they see themselves as having beyond the TCO?

The management of the revenues derived from resource extraction in the Chaco remains an unresolved problem. As we have seen, Tarija is not short of cash, nor are some of the municipalities of the Chaco region. Attempts have been made at redistribution within the department of Tarija, most notably to the benefit of the peasant population in the department through the Prosol scheme and through special funding for municipalities. Some of the profits have been used to improve education and health provision. But even within municipalities, as we saw in the case of Villamontes, egregious inequalities stand out. And, as is the case in most resource-rich jurisdictions anywhere in the world, it is difficult to ensure that the benefits are adequately divided up between competing claimants. This is particularly the case when the reach of the state is only partial. Also, where the state is weak and prone to corrupt behaviour, rents are easily channelled off into private pockets. Managing the resources from resource booms is never easy, but much more attention needs to be paid, at various levels of government, to ensure a fairer distribution of the benefits. Without it, political conflict will remain a perennial problem, affecting not least the region's increasingly empowered indigenous populations.

7 | SANTA CRUZ AND THE PROCESS OF CHANGE

The development of Santa Cruz

Far from the main sources of minerals in Bolivia, Santa Cruz grew up isolated from the rest of the country, an agricultural town serving its immediate hinterland. Its economic importance – at least that of the department of Santa Cruz, Bolivia's largest – was enhanced by the building of rail connections with Brazil to the east and Argentina to the south in the early twentieth century along with the development of the oil industry in the mid-1920s, especially in and around the town of Camiri in the south of the department. But until the 1950s, with the construction of the road to Cochabamba, when the city of Santa Cruz was physically linked with the rest of Bolivia, the department remained something of an economic backwater, a recipient of resources from the central government in La Paz based on revenues from the mining industry. In 1950, Santa Cruz had less than 10 per cent of Bolivia's total population. The physiognomy of the city was a criss-cross of narrow earthen streets stretching out from its substantial central plaza, with modest one-storey buildings with their typical wooden colonnades and covered walkways providing passers-by with shelter from the extremes of tropical sun and rain. Beyond the immediate confines of the city, agricultural activities predominated, largely serving the local urban market. Apart from a few small towns, built around mission settlements created in the eighteenth century by Jesuit communities, the greater part of the department of Santa Cruz was virgin land inhabited by indigenous peoples, the Chiquitanos, the Guarayos, the Ayoreos and the Guaraníes.

The economic take-off of Santa Cruz dates from the late 1950s and 1960s. The influential Bohan Plan of 1940, the outcome of a US advisory programme, had pointed to the importance of commercial agriculture in any strategy of economic diversification in Bolivia. The pattern of development adopted in these years focused on cash crops, mainly for export, such as sugar and cotton, for which processing involved a nascent industrialization. There was also the expansion of huge extensions of land devoted to cattle-rearing, often at the expense of indigenous communities. The governments of the time sought to use the development of agriculture to ease land constraints on the Altiplano by encouraging migration. Colonization settlements such as San Julián and Yapacaní to the north of Santa Cruz attracted large numbers of peasants who brought their culture and traditions of organization with them. Migrants also provided a cheap labour force on large agricultural estates. In the agricultural sphere, therefore, landholding developed along two distinct paths: the multiplication of small-scale peasant holdings, particularly in the region north and north-west of Santa Cruz city, and to the south-west; elsewhere, immense landed estates – often several hundred thousand hectares in area – multiplied, their owners taking advantage of the apparent abundance of available land. Meanwhile, the indigenous peoples of Santa Cruz, ill prepared to defend their land from outsiders, found their habitat under increasing threat. The expansion of agribusiness in Santa Cruz owed much to the military government of General Hugo Banzer (1971–78), under whose aegis large amounts of land were distributed to his supporters (Banzer came originally from Concepción in Santa Cruz) and copious bank credit extended to large landholders there (most of it never to be repaid).

The development of Santa Cruz at this time also saw the growth of other economic sectors, notably hydrocarbons and drugs. The first of these, which had stagnated following the first oil boom of the 1920s, saw new growth in both oil and gas development. By the end of the 1970s, natural gas exports (to Argentina) had overtaken tin as Bolivia's prime source of export revenue. At much the same time, the generation of revenues from cocaine base became a new source of wealth (albeit illicit) in Santa Cruz. Although coca was not cultivated in Santa Cruz, drug manufacturing and dealing interests took root in the department. During the short-lived government of General Luis García Meza (1980–81), when drug interests seized political control of the country, one of Santa Cruz's top drug barons, Roberto Suárez, publicly offered to pay off Bolivia's foreign debt from his own back pocket.

The growth in wealth of Santa Cruz during this period led to the rapid expansion of the city, attracting large numbers of immigrants. Some came from the rural hinterland but most from the highlands. In 1950, the city had a population of roughly 43,000; in 2001 it stood at over 1.1 million, and eleven years on at around 1.8 million. The old city centre, surrounded by its circular ring road (or *anillo*), grew rapidly into new surrounding neighbourhoods, some noteworthy for their opulence, others equally noteworthy for their poor housing and poverty. The number of concentric *anillos* grew. By the early 1980s there were four *anillos*; today there are eight or more. The map of Santa Cruz gives the impression of a planned city, with its radiating avenues and circular *anillos*. The reality is anything but, according to Fernando Prado, a leading *cruceño* architect. The patterns of population growth, accompanied by a liberal laissez-faire attitude among the city fathers, have led to the concentration of resources in the central areas, and beyond to a chaotic growth, contamination and an urban infrastructure simply unable to cope.

Politically, Santa Cruz – at least its elites and middle class – has long been noted for its conservatism. During the 1950s, Santa Cruz was the centre for opposition to the then reformist MNR governments, and a bastion for the quasi-fascist Falange Socialista Boliviana (FSB). The FSB used Santa Cruz to launch a short-lived guerrilla campaign against the revolutionary government for which it paid a heavy price. Later, the right-wing Banzer government drew much of its political support from Santa Cruz, a department whose elites (as we have seen) benefited greatly from its land and credit policies. Santa Cruz provided the base for Banzer's attempt in the 1980s to build a political party, the Acción Democrática Nacionalista (ADN). The political elites tended to make use of a strong dose of regionalist sentiment to cement their control.

A consequence of the growth of the *cruceño* economy was the development of a number of powerful local institutions: the Cámara Agropecuaria del Oriente (CAO) representing agribusiness; the Federación de Ganaderos de Santa Cruz (Fegasacruz), the cattle rearers; the Cámara de Industria y Comercio (CAINCO), industrial and commercial interests; and the Cámara de Hidrocarburos y Energía, the oil and gas industry. At the apex of these various sectoral institutions was the civic committee (of which they were prime members and funders), the Comité Pro Santa Cruz. Though all Bolivia's nine departments have civic committees, none achieved the power and influence wielded by the Comité Pro Santa Cruz. It has seen its role as defending the interests and autonomy of Santa Cruz against centralizing governments in La Paz. Over the years, this has led to various threats of separatism. Conservative networks among the *cruceño* elite have also long been reinforced by semi-secret societies or *logias* whose members include many well-placed (exclusively male) members of high society. Two *logias* have predominated: the Toborochi and the Caballeros del Oriente. The *logias* have long exercised strong control over local institutions, notably a number of highly profitable public service cooperatives. Another influential local institution, a spin-off from the Comité Pro Santa Cruz, is the Unión Juvenil Cruceñista (UJC), a paramilitary youth organization that directs itself against those it perceives as 'enemies' of *la cruceñidad*.

The world of the *cruceño* elites has long been notable for its exclusivity. There are a number of social clubs whose members are chosen on the basis of their surnames. 'These are circles of people who are *cruceños* by birth,' says Isaac Sandoval Rodríguez, a leading local historian. 'Your surname is everything,' says Hugo Salvatierra, a *cruceño* leader of the MAS who became agriculture minister in Morales's first administration; 'this is not a class, but a caste.' Control of organizations like the CAO and the service cooperatives, not to mention the Comité Pro Santa Cruz, has always been restricted to those from well-established *cruceño* families. The only newcomers to these circles of power tended to be those from immigrant families from abroad, many of them German or eastern European in origin. Closely related to this exclusivity has been a xenophobic attitude towards migrants from other parts of the country, particularly from the highlands. The so-called '*kollas*' have not had a look-in when it comes to membership of key local institutions. This has given rise to the duality of '*cambas*' and '*kollas*', *cambas* being the name taken by those born and bred in Santa Cruz. It is perhaps ironic that originally *cambas* were indigenous people, a far cry from the white supremacists who promote organizations like the UJC and who like to project what they call the Nación Camba.

The rise of the MAS as a powerful electoral force in Santa Cruz provided a direct challenge to the traditional power structure dominated by the right. Its electoral strength lay almost entirely in those sectors of the population of Santa Cruz that were migrants from other parts of Bolivia, especially the highlands. Barred from elite politics, these were people without a political voice. 'The *kollas* found refuge in the MAS,' says Salvatierra, who notes that on the party's departmental executive committee he was the only one actually born in Santa Cruz. 'All the rest were *kollas*,' he says. But such was the demographic dynamic of *kollas* in Santa Cruz department – especially in colonization zones and in low-income urban neighbourhoods – that the MAS quickly found it had a strong presence. In provinces like Ichilo, Ñuflo de Chávez and Caballero, peasants and *colonizadores* eagerly voted for the MAS. Over the department as a whole, the MAS vote increased from just over 10 per cent in the 2002 presidential elections to over 33 per cent in 2005 (and over 40 per cent in 2009). Even in the urban population of Santa Cruz city in 2005, more than 30 per cent voted for the MAS. The idea of the '*media luna*' – counterposing the MAS-dominated western, highland departments against the opposition-led lowland ones – was something of a myth.

The electoral victory of Evo Morales in 2005 and the extremely poor showing of traditional conservative parties came as a severe shock to the *cruceño* establishment. As in the past, its response was to rally local opinion around the notion of autonomy, questioning the power of central government and using this to mobilize opinion against the MAS government and the Constituent Assembly. Hostility to the draft constitution and fears about restrictions on landholding drove the Comité Pro Santa Cruz, supported by local institutions, into a position in 2007/08 that came close to declaring de facto independence from La Paz. The statute of autonomy, drafted by the Comité and approved by a large majority in a local referendum in May 2008, was an open statement of defiance against the national government. In the violence that followed in August and September 2008, leading political figures in Santa Cruz openly and violently defied the authority of the central government. Graffiti on the walls in central Santa Cruz threatened Evo Morales with death should he dare set foot in Santa Cruz. State institutions were ransacked. But, as we shall see, the degree of violence and the brazen and racist behaviour of organizations like the UJC helped tip the political balance back in the Morales government's favour. Still, the potency of the threat of secession was such as to convince Morales and others in government of the need to embrace the idea of autonomy and to incorporate it – in one way or another – in the new constitution.

Changes in the structure of power

The violence that erupted in Santa Cruz and other cities in eastern Bolivia in September 2008 came to represent a watershed in the conflictive relations between the lowland elites and the government in La Paz. Previously in Santa Cruz, Rubén Costas, the departmental prefect elected in 2006, with the support of the Comité Pro Santa Cruz, had been able to mobilize opinion around the issue of autonomy. However, the scale of the violence made many think twice about the kind of tactics being used by the political elite. The business community, in particular, began to look askance at these activities, seeing little to be gained from such brazen opposition to the government. Internationally, too, the episode showed that there was absolutely no appetite elsewhere in Latin America for supporting a campaign for anything that even resembled secession by violent means. Costas and his friends, it seemed, had overplayed their hand – and badly. The September violence thus provided Evo Morales with an opportunity to wrest back the political initiative, driving a wedge between the political opposition over the vexed issue of the constitution and opening up new possibilities for dialogue with the powerful business organizations of Santa Cruz.

A supposed international 'terrorist' plot the following year in Santa Cruz involved a motley bunch of mainly European malcontents and some former mercenaries from the Balkan wars. This provided the opportunity further to question a number of influential figures – not least the then president of the Comité Pro Santa Cruz, Branko Marinkovic, a large landowner of Croatian descent. The exact motives and objectives of those immediately involved remained unclear at the time of writing, and an official inquiry was still under way. Three of the five at the centre of the plot were killed in an assault on a Santa Cruz hotel. The main political significance of this was the accusation that the 'terrorists' had been invited to Bolivia and funded and organized by key figures of the *cruceño* elite. According to one interpretation, their objective had been to assassinate Morales and members of his government. Others within Santa Cruz affirm that the whole operation had been a put-up job, organized by the government to discredit members of the political opposition in Santa Cruz. Whatever the truth, the incident cast serious aspersions as to the political motivations of important political figures within Santa Cruz. Marinkovic, for one, escaped to Brazil shortly afterwards. According to Helena Argirakis, a leading analyst of *cruceño* politics, the violence of September 2008, followed by the 2009 'terrorist plot', sealed the fate of those who held out for radical autonomy. 'They underestimated the force of the state, of the government, and of Evo Morales,' she says.

The December 2009 presidential elections effectively further neutralized the power of the right-wing opposition in Santa Cruz. The MAS in 2009 won over 40 per cent of the vote in the presidential elections in the department as a whole, with as much as 72 per cent in Ichilo, a province with a large population of *colonizadores*, and well over 50 per cent in several others. Two of the four seats in the Senate for Santa Cruz went to MAS candidates. Although Costas was elected governor in the local elections of April 2010, the MAS was able (in conjunction with indigenous representatives in the departmental assembly) to win 14 of the 28 assembly seats. At the level of local government, 26 of the 52 municipalities in Santa Cruz department went to the MAS. Moreover, with the passage of the constitution and its provisions for autonomies on up to four different levels (departmental, municipal, indigenous and regional), this powerful mobilizing issue in *cruceño* politics was to a certain extent neutralized, even though the degree of autonomy conceded was nowhere near so far reaching as that contemplated by the 2008 statutes of autonomy approved by referendums in Santa Cruz, as well as in the Beni, Pando and Tarija. Finally, the leverage that Costas was able to exert in the '*media luna*' was greatly reduced by the elimination of key allies: in 2009 the governor of Pando was imprisoned for his supposed role in the killing of sixteen peasants there the year before; in 2010 the governor of Tarija went into self-imposed exile in Paraguay following accusations of serious corruption; and in 2012, the governor of Beni was suspended following accusations of improper use of public funds. As for Costas himself, he faced a number of judicial accusations, not least the use of public funds to finance the 'illegal' referendum on departmental autonomies in 2008. According to Argirakis, the political elite – led by the governor and the mayor – simply failed to see how things had changed in Santa Cruz. 'Bolivia, the world, the region had all moved on,' she says, 'but they continued to manage public affairs as if this [Santa Cruz] was their personal fiefdom.'

While it is difficult to draw a clear dividing line between the activities of political and economic elites in Santa Cruz, one of the changes to come about since 2008 has been the relative acquiescence of the latter to the plans and policies of the government. According to Salvatierra, 'ideologically they are against the government, but in terms of policy they support it'. There remains some disagreement as to the extent of and the reasons behind this détente, but – broadly speaking – it seems that business groups in Santa Cruz have been relatively happy with the economic policies pursued by the Morales administration. According to Carlos Hugo Molina, a former departmental prefect (under the government of Carlos Mesa), 'from 2008 onwards, there has been a separation of the political from the economic; there has been a tsunami which has changed everything'. Rapid growth rates, accompanied by low levels of inflation, have fostered a positive business climate in which healthy profits can be made. Molina argues that while the business groups make money, they are doing so with the approval of the government. Meanwhile, he says, they have largely stopped funding the Comité Pro Santa Cruz, plunging this once all-powerful institution into a financial crisis.

Macroeconomic stability has certainly favoured the banking industry, which is rooted in Santa Cruz. The soya industry has benefited from years of relatively high prices and government supports. The hydrocarbons industry has also seen increases in output, which, while primarily benefiting Tarija, have also brought economic dividends to Santa Cruz. The business sector 'is much better off today than they were under Goni', says Salvatierra. Finally, the narcotics industry appears to have expanded in recent years. The available evidence suggests that cocaine production and trafficking have both tracked upwards, even though (as we saw in Chapter 5) coca production has not increased substantially. According to Alejandro Dausá from Desafío, a local urban development NGO in Santa Cruz, 'there is considerable local affluence, there's no shortage of money around [...] drugs move more money than soya'. Meanwhile, as we shall see, the agrarian and agribusiness elites seem to have found a modus vivendi with the Morales government which protects them from the threat of radical land redistribution and provides the basis for assured markets for their products, both internally and abroad.

The relative prosperity of Santa Cruz in recent years has not been entirely confined to elites; it has had significant trickle-down effects among less prosperous sectors of the population as well. While formal-sector employment has not increased greatly, there has been a rapid expansion in the informal sector, focused on sectors such as construction and services. Wages in construction have increased substantially. While a building labourer could expect to earn 30 bolivianos a day (some US$5) in 2007, by 2012 the rates were around 90 bolivianos (including an element for lunch). A skilled builder could expect to earn 150 bolivianos and a contractor 300 bolivianos. Similarly, there has been significant growth in the transport sector, particularly in employment for drivers and mechanics. In agriculture too, though jobs tend to be temporary (for the sowing season and for the harvest), people have managed to find work. Contraband activities have prospered, with imports largely from Argentina. 'The black economy moves a lot of money,' says Dausá at Desafío. 'We notice that there has been an increase in the money in people's pockets,' says Juan José Avila, also from Desafío, 'improving their ability to buy land in places like Pailón' (situated to the east of Santa Cruz city across the Río Grande). Marfa Silva, a local leader from the low-income Plan 3000 district, agrees: 'economically, we're much more stable; people's incomes have improved'. She has spent time working in Argentina, where prices are very high. 'At least you can get a lunch here for US$1.50,' she adds.

In spite of the relatively muted impact in Santa Cruz of changes observable elsewhere in Bolivia, significant changes have taken place in the department, many of which may be difficult to reverse. With *kollas* representing around half the population of the department, the ability of the *cruceño* elite to maintain its traditional control over the department's politics has been cast into considerable doubt. The relative prosperity of Santa Cruz and its ability to provide employment of sorts will mean that it will continue to attract migratory flows from the rest of the country. Both among urban populations and migrant communities in rural areas, there are processes of economic accumulation. These are often the sectors of the population which work hardest and for longest hours, particularly in commerce, managing to save a proportion of what they earn. 'There may not be a change in the productive model,' says Juan José Avila, 'but there are new groups that are quite comfortably off, which think they belong here [...] there are *nouveaux riches* keen to get on board.' And though there remain institutions, such as the exclusive Club Social 24 de Septiembre, which are off limits to those not born and bred in Santa Cruz, other once exclusive spaces – like the University Gabriel René Moreno – are opening their doors to the city's new citizens. 'This is part of the new Bolivia [...] it's a melting pot,' Isaac Sandóval remarks.

The changing face of agriculture

The road east from Santa Cruz towards the Chiquitanía crosses flat agricultural land, fields of soya and sunflower stretching out as far (indeed, much farther) than the eye can see. Billboards proclaim the virtues of genetically modified seed and of chemical fertilizers and pesticides, messages which the farmers here have evidently taken to heart; nearly all Bolivian soya production is now GM. Where small-scale producers were dominant thirty years ago, larger extensions of land now prevail. San Julián is a poignant example. This is an area of colonization where in the late 1970s migrants from Potosí and other highland departments hacked a living out of the forest, clearing their 50-hectare plots of land to plant maize, yuca and a few vegetables. Today there is only the suggestion of forest, a few islands of trees in a sea of soya. Commercial agriculture is king here. Even among the *colonizadores* there has been some concentration of ownership, as the stronger producers appropriate the land of the weaker, the latter turning instead to commerce, transport and moving to other points on the agricultural frontier.

The expansion of 'modern' agriculture has brought major changes to the agricultural scene in Santa Cruz, with large-scale, highly mechanized forms of production taking centre stage, particularly in the north-eastern part of the department, where land has traditionally been plentiful and cheap. Here soya rules supreme, produced in large part for export, most of it not as a raw commodity but in processed form. Soya accounts for well over half of the value of agro-industrial production in Santa Cruz. The industry has attracted major interest from foreigners – primarily Brazilians, but also Argentines, Paraguayans and Chileans attracted by the low cost of land and the large profits to be made. Bolivia has traditionally sold most of its soya to Colombia under preferential rules agreed within the Andean Community of Nations (CAN), but has more recently found new markets in Venezuela.

However, oil seed production coexists with other more traditional agricultural practices. To the north of Santa Cruz – primarily in places like Yapacaní and San Julián – small-scale *colonizadores* have grown crops like rice, sugar cane and cotton, although soya is taking over here, and is spreading northwards up towards the Beni. And as we have seen, many are not so small-scale, with 'small producers' having properties of well over two hundred hectares. In the valleys to the south-west of Santa Cruz, much smaller-scale peasant production still prevails with the cultivation of vegetables and citrus fruit for the domestic market. Farther south, in the province of Cordillera on the fringes of the Chaco, cattle raising predominates, often on vast estates, as is also the case in large parts of the Chiquitanía that are unsuited to the production of soya, but where timber from the forest is also big business.

But it is soya, more than anything else, which has exerted increasing pressure on landholding, pushing into areas previously dominated by indigenous and peasant producers. Problems of landlessness are in the ascendant, with the children of original peasant settlers unable to find land to cultivate. At the same time, indigenous peoples are losing the land which is recognized as theirs. According to Hugo Salvatierra, it is giving rise 'to an explosive situation, and in the short term'. The expansion of the agricultural frontier is also having other negative consequences. According to Eulogio Núñez, at

CIPCA in Santa Cruz, between 250,000 and 300,000 hectares of forest are being cleared – principally in the north of the Chiquitanía and in Guarayos – each year, primarily to give way to soya. 'Agribusiness is doing away with the Amazon forest,' he says. Since this is land that is unsuited to intensive farming, it is creating major problems of soil degradation. Núñez points to the failure to observe even basic techniques to avoid wind erosion, such as tree blocks, that help conserve soils and prevent sedimentation of the river systems. 'We have comparatively quite a lot of forest cover left,' he says, 'but at this rate it won't last long.' Miguel Angel Crespo at Probioma, an NGO in Santa Cruz that promotes techniques to protect biodiversity, is particularly damning in his appraisal of the use of chemical fertilizers and genetically modified seed. He quotes figures that show how the use of GM seed in the soya industry increased from 40 per cent in 2006 to 98 per cent in 2011, and how in 2000 12 kilograms of agro-chemicals were used per hectare, increasing to 54 kilograms in 2011. Among those who have destroyed the forest, Núñez cites the Mennonites, an extreme Protestant religious sect of Germanic origin whose numbers have increased substantially in the last twenty years. 'They are like termites,' he says.

Government attempts to regularize landownership in Santa Cruz through *saneamiento* have been less successful than in many other parts of the country, mainly because of resistance from established landowners, particularly in the Chiquitanía and in Cordillera province. Of a total of 106 million hectares of land subject to *saneamiento* nationally, 61 million had been *saneado* at the end of 2011. Fear among landed interests that *saneamiento* would be a prelude to redistribution seems to have dissipated over time, particularly as the process of land titling lost its original impetus by 2010. The 2009 referendum on landownership, which took place at the same time as the constitutional referendum, reaffirmed an upward limit of 5,000 hectares on land being used for productive purposes, but this was not made retroactive. Many landowners in Santa Cruz have estates that far exceed this limit.

For observers like Salvatierra, the only answer to the pressure on the land is not titling but redistribution in favour of those most in need. The amount of land redistributed in Santa Cruz in recent years has been small. Some of those most intimately involved in land regulation in the early years of the Morales government fear that the tide of land redistribution has turned definitively. Juan Carlos Rojas, who headed up the INRA from 2006 to 2010, is of the opinion that 'the process of community-based land distribution is now closed', likening this to the way in which the MNR governments of the 1950s retreated from the objectives of the 1953 land reform. 'My big worry is that the cycle has ended,' he says, pointing to the negotiations between government officials and organizations representing large landowners and agro-industrial interests. He argues that the government's December 2011 summit, bringing together different civil society groups in Cochabamba, represented a further retreat from the objectives of land reform. This was attended by business organizations, including those of landed interests. They sought to ease the rules regarding the productive use of land. Other observers point to the maintenance of important privileges for the *cruceño* farming community, such as the provision of subsidized diesel and the ability to negotiate export quotas and thereby benefit from higher international prices for products like vegetable oil than those available domestically.

Those working for NGOs involved in agricultural issues stress a pivotal shift in government policy, particularly as the government entered its second term at the beginning of 2010. While Eulogio Núñez at CIPCA sees the 2009 constitution's commitment to a 'plural economy' as 'new and innovative', he sees the state as siding increasingly with export-oriented agribusiness interests in Santa Cruz at the expense of the constitutional commitment to 'sustainable rural development'. 'We think there should be respect for the sustainability of the soil,' he says, accusing the state agency Empresa de Apoyo a la Producción de Alimentos, Emapa, of promoting genetically modified soya production. He sees the contradiction between sustainable patterns of agricultural development and the promotion of agro-industry as the 'root issue' at stake in the TIPNIS dispute. Similarly, Alcides Vadillo, at the Fundación Tierra in Santa Cruz, points to changes in government discourse from one of 'agrarian revolution' (relating to land reform) in 2006 to one of a 'productive revolution' in 2011. Vadillo, who worked previously as an adviser to the Cidob, sees as the reason for this the recognition of Santa Cruz as the source of 75 per cent of the food consumed in Bolivia. Of this 82 per cent is produced by agro-industry. Spurred on by a fall in agricultural production in 2007 and the rise in international food prices the following year with consequent inflationary pressures, 'the government reconsidered the role of agro-industry in the national economy', he says. For his part, Miguel Angel Crespo at Probioma reckons that Santa Cruz accounts for 93 per cent of meat production, 63 per cent of milk, 63 per cent of fruit and even 45 per cent of potatoes. With a growing urban population, it is perhaps unsurprising that guaranteeing supplies of food (and thus lower prices) has become a more central preoccupation for those in government.

Several of those we talked to were thus sceptical about the extent to which government policy had shifted from the neoliberal model it inherited. 'We do not see economic management ending the neoliberal vision of things,' says Gualberto Flores from Foro Vecinal, a neighbourhood organization in Santa Cruz. Alcides Vadillo agrees, suggesting that while there has been no change in the model, there has been a change 'in those who administer it', pointing to greater state involvement in the productive process. This has tended to focus on support for smaller-scale producers, in the provision of credit, the building of new storage facilities and the development of new markets for their produce through Emapa, the state purchasing agency. These innovations, however, do not appear to have been wholly successful. The provision of credit through Emapa for small-scale producers of rice, sugar, maize and soya in the north of Santa Cruz was not always forthcoming when producers most needed it. Price supports for rice producers backfired when such steps resulted in overproduction. Provision of seed and fertilizer by Emapa to small-scale producers at times ended up causing substantial problems when it arrived late. Agreements to purchase agricultural produce frequently became entangled with bureaucracy, while, as signs along the road to San Julián show, private intermediaries will pay cash on delivery with no questions asked.

Despite such problems, however, the economic situation affecting small-scale producers appears to have improved substantially since 2006. In Vadillo's opinion, 'the campesino is in a better situation than five years ago; he has access to land, credit and machinery'. Certainly some small-scale producers have been able to graduate to a much bigger league, taking full advantage of the opportunities open to them. There has also been greater participation in spheres of decision-making which represent an important break from the past, challenging the control traditionally exercised by business elites. An iconic (though perhaps atypical) example of this is the fact that the president of Anapo, the national oilseed producers' association, a powerful voice in the world of agribusiness, is Demetrio Pérez, a small-scale producer whose family hails from rural Potosí. 'Choosing such a person to negotiate with the Morales administration was one of the smartest moves they could have made,' says Miguel Angel Crespo. The world of agribusiness appears to have come to an amicable modus vivendi with the Morales administration, although not without breeding a climate of resentment between the government and some of its allies.

Social organization in the rural sphere has also advanced in recent years, taking advantage of the increased spaces afforded to defend popular interests. A key development here was probably the Bloque Oriente, established in 2001, bringing together indigenous, peasant, rural labourer and landless groups with urban groups like Foro Vecinal. Social movements largely supported the election of Evo Morales and the process of reformulating the constitution so as to reflect their interests. Like other social movement organizations, the Bloque has suffered internal tensions and splits, but it has managed to survive intact, promoting areas of common concern. In 2012, these included working on the elaboration of plans for departmental autonomy. However, as elsewhere and particularly since 2010, the divisions between peasants and indigenous organizations over different visions of development (and particularly the mobilization over the TIPNIS dispute) weakened this sense of unity between sectors, and indeed encouraged divisions between them. As of mid-2012, most of the social organizations in Santa Cruz, particularly in the indigenous sphere, had suffered internal splits, some of them violent, over their support for (or rejection of) the Morales government and its policies on the TIPNIS issue.

The other side of town

Entering the northern suburbs of Santa Cruz city gives the impression of unbridled wealth, with car dealerships selling the latest in glitzy motors, fast-food outlets and large supermarkets offering a universe of consumer goods, but there is a very different reality in other parts of town. Visit the south-eastern districts of Villa Primero de Mayo (District 6), San Aurelio (District 12) and Plan 3000 (District 8), Cotoca to the east, or District 9 to the south-west of the city, and you find yourself in what are typical Latin American slum settlements. Of these, Plan 3000 is the largest. It has a population of between 300,000 and 400,000 people (the November 2012 census promised to provide a more accurate figure); as much as a fifth of the city's total population lives there.

Plan 3000 came into being thirty years ago, in 1983, when freak storms caused the River Piraí to burst its banks and send flood waters into the poverty-stricken communities in this low-lying part of the city. The disaster occurred on 13 March, a date recalled with grief every year since then. Three thousand families were supposedly affected, hence the name. The families affected were initially given shelter in the university, and then 'relocated' to an uncultivated area on the periphery. 'They treated us as if we weren't human beings,' says Marfa Silva; 'they simply disposed of us without food or water to this piece of unused land. [...] if we were poor before, here we had no services whatsoever.' She recalls how the local landowner refused to allow them access to his tap. According to Edwin Grimaldo, headmaster of St Andrew's College, a school in Plan 3000, much of the international aid raised to help the flood victims disappeared in official corruption. Families initially lived in tents, and were then offered plots for which they were charged 2,000 bolivianos but to which they were never given title deeds. 'It was daylight robbery,' in Grimaldo's view.

To reach Plan 3000, a brand-new dual carriageway leads out from the city centre with street lighting and ornamental palm trees, but the road stops abruptly before you reach the township. You plunge leftwards down an earthen track with large potholes before eventually emerging by the market, the area where Plan 3000 first took shape in 1983. The day we visited, the rain poured down, turning the streets into a muddy morass. Buses plied their way through the mud, carrying their human cargo towards the city centre, some five kilometres distant, with scant concern for the pedestrians on the roadside close by. There is little by way of work or amenities in Plan 3000. Most people work in the city. The main sources of employment are the sort of commercial activities that characterize most urban settlements in Bolivia. The district grew up in an unplanned way, largely ignored by the municipal authorities in Santa Cruz.

Since 1983, Plan 3000 has become a first port of call for migrants from all over Bolivia. 'The speed at which people have come has been surprising,' says Marfa Silva, one of its original settlers. 'It's like Bolivia in miniature,' says Edwin Grimaldo; 'there are miners from Oruro, black people from the Yungas, even *"ponchos rojos"*[1] from Achacachi.' Organizationally, people came together around the demand for basic services. In 1989, there were protest marches to demand electricity and water. Grimaldo recalls how 5,000 people marched to the centre of Santa Cruz, the Plaza 24 de Septiembre. According to Eduardo Correa, a recent sub-mayor of Plan 3000, 'people come together when there is a need'. This was the case, for example, in 2008, when in the heat of the conflicts with the government, the right-wing Unión Juvenil Cruceñista sought to attack what it perceived as a bastion of the MAS. UJC supporters tried to burn down the market in Plan 3000, but were beaten off by the locals. Grimaldo remembers how, rallied by appeals over the local radio, some 20,000 people came out 'to defend their stalls in the market'. Eduardo Loayza, who works in the community radio in Plan 3000, comments how in 'moments of struggle, the radio plays a key role'.

However, the achievement of basic services has reduced levels of collective action. 'People get used to the little they have,' says Correa; 'if they have electricity and water and a means of transport, they think they have it all.' Also rivalries between different community leaders and the removal of constant external threats have made it difficult to sustain organizational unity across the district. Gualberto Flores from Foro Vecinal stresses how lack of unity makes it difficult to work

---

1 Those who wear the red ponchos typical of many parts of the northern Altiplano.

there and how competing external actors make this worse. 'Everyone, the municipality [of Santa Cruz], the local governor and his office, the central government [in La Paz] all want to involve themselves [...] there is a lack of coordination, sticking plaster remedies, and a lot of co-optation.' Correa recounts how the electoral weight of Plan 3000 means that it is seen as an important political resource. 'Some support Evo, others Percy [Fernández, the mayor of Santa Cruz] [...] it's a dirty way of conducting politics that takes advantage of the fact that people are poorly informed.' For his part, José Chávez, a local community leader, decries the way in which the *juntas vecinales* – there is one in each of the 127 sub-districts – fail to project the views and aspirations of those they supposedly represent. 'Our leaders simply turn their backs on us,' he remarks, alluding to the fact that they are often bought off by outsiders, particularly by the municipality. Grimaldo puts it more forcefully: 'they [the *dirigentes*] are bought off by food, drink and sex'.

Though most voted enthusiastically for the MAS in the presidential elections of 2005 and again in 2009, we noted a mood of disillusion on which opponents of the ruling party have been able to capitalize. 'There were a lot of high expectations,' says Grimaldo, who, despite reservations, continues to support the MAS locally, 'and now people in the MAS have fallen out fighting for jobs in government.' Correa puts it starkly: 'people sell themselves for a bowl of rice', he says. Correa is also a MAS supporter who was forced to resign as sub-mayor in 2011 because of confrontations with Mayor Percy Fernández, whose office made it impossible to carry out his job. Support for the MAS appears also to have diminished since the confrontations of 2008. Up until then, backing the party was the only way to express opposition to the Comité Pro Santa Cruz and the interests it represented. Up until 2008, the Bloque Oriente broadly endorsed the policies of the MAS and the rewriting of the constitution. Since then, the Bloque has undergone divisions, particularly between the peasants and *colonizadores* on the one hand (who support the MAS) and the indigenous organizations (such as Cidob) on the other. The local union movement, represented by the Central Obrera Departamental (COD), has also undergone internal splits over recent years.

Still, many of the locals we spoke to pointed to improvements that have come about as a result of policies of the Morales government. Improvements in education are widely appreciated, particularly the building of new schools in Plan 3000. The Juancito Pinto allowance (directed towards schoolchildren) appears to have reduced levels of school absenteeism and the abandonment of education altogether, particularly by girls. Correa points to the school building programme in Plan 3000, as well as to the fact that people are no longer charged to graduate when they have completed secondary education. 'In spite of the number of classrooms built, there are still not enough,' he says, 'and we're still not providing a truly free education.' For her part, Marfa Silva points to improvements in water supplies, and in particular to a scheme to put in main drainage and sewerage, a plan funded by the central government and the Inter-American Development Bank (IDB). 'This is very important for us,' she says. Since 2004, Marfa has been involved as president of the local water cooperative, one of the few women in the neighbourhood to take up this sort of position. She also draws attention to the positive results of the Renta Dignidad programme for the elderly: 'there's no longer such a problem of old people being abandoned', she comments.

Life in Plan 3000, despite the thirty years of the district's existence, remains precarious for most. Problems of underemployment and low income remain widespread, as do the social problems that arise from poverty. The population profile is very young, with as much as half under the age of twenty-five. Large numbers of young people therefore enter the labour force each year, with little or no hope of achieving stable or reasonably paid work. Informal activities, such as those in the service and commerce sectors, tend to provide scant income. Life is also made precarious by the prevalence of crime and the lack of a police presence to confront it. According to Eduardo Correa, there are only 150 policemen in the whole of Plan 3000, including those that do not patrol the streets, for an area with a population approaching 400,000. Furthermore, and despite the passage of time, only a small proportion of the population has had the money or connections to negotiate titles for the land they occupy. Some remain in hock financially to the original owners of the land that they first settled in 1983. 'Lack of a title makes it impossible to get credit, to borrow money,' says Marfa Silva; 'we also need land titles if we want to pass on our homes to our children when we die.' A law passed by the government in 2012 may go some way to solving this problem by enabling people to get titles when they can show they have occupied a plot for at least five years. Sixty per cent of those living in Plan 3000 lack land titles.

Resolving these sorts of issues remains a major challenge for the people of Plan 3000 and other low-income districts in Santa Cruz. The lack of permanent and strong organizational networks certainly does not help. People find it difficult to force the authorities, whether at departmental or national level, to respond to their problems. The scope for popular participation over decision-making at the local level is very limited, and the relationship between the municipality of Santa Cruz and the *juntas vecinales* in Plan 3000 and other districts is highly clientelistic. 'Neither the municipality nor the *gobernación* are politically accountable,' says Gualberto Flores at Foro Vecinal, set up in 2008 precisely to push for more accountability and greater public participation in local government in the poorer parts of Santa Cruz. A long-running objective of leaders in Plan 3000 has been to set up a local municipality, independent of Santa Cruz, following the example pioneered by El Alto in the 1990s. But this appears to be a non-starter. 'The government has failed to use decree laws to do this,' says José Chavez, a supporter of Foro Vecinal in Plan 3000, and 'to engage with the *gobernación* on such matters is to enter a bureaucratic labyrinth'.

Conclusions

Traditionally, Santa Cruz has been one of Bolivia's most conservative departments. Its politics have been dominated by a relatively small but hugely powerful group of families who have tended to monopolize its main institutions, both political and economic. The dominant ideology among this group has been one of proud defence of the perceived interests of Santa Cruz, as against interference from the centralizing tendencies of government in La Paz – especially when those governments were of a leftist nature. That dominance may now be in question. The political and business elites no longer sing from quite the same hymn sheet. The violence that took place in Santa Cruz and the concern of the Morales administration to ensure that such violence is not repeated have led to something of an entente between the main business organizations (and their members) and the government. The much-trumpeted campaign for regional autonomy has fizzled out, suggesting that resisting policies emanating from La Paz was never the true motive; the real reason for the mobilization in 2008 was defence of Santa Cruz from the threat to its productive system, based on *latifundio* farming and agribusiness. By 2012, that threat was no longer so much on the minds of business organizations. With business thriving under the MAS administration, the old methods of achieving their interests seemed less effective. For its part, the once powerful Comité Pro Santa Cruz was left bereft, deprived of the committed support of its erstwhile backers. The political elite thus found itself reduced to a rump. As one of our interviewees put it, it consisted only of the mayor, the governor, the cardinal and the media. However, the extent to which this change consolidates itself will depend crucially on how divergent groups within the old elite behave, whether those in power continue to choose to play ball with the MAS, and whether emerging new actors manage to play a bigger role.

In this context, new sectors were emerging in *cruceño* society, a far more complex and multifaceted society than thirty years before. With around half the population of *kolla* origin, migrants from the highlands or their offspring, it was no longer possible to maintain a society in which these were effectively marginalized and excluded. Townships at the periphery of Santa Cruz city, such as that of Plan 3000, were becoming increasingly restive, dissatisfied by the poor attention they receive from the authorities, particularly the mayor. They found themselves able to mobilize, to vote in authorities of their own, non-aligned with the traditional political elites. New economic sectors emerged, dominated by immigrants to the city. They brought with them many of the organizational traditions that have characterized other parts of Bolivia. And their organizations, whether in rural or urban areas, have become more assertive, less willing to submit to previously dominant local organizations. This is not something that will easily be reversed. Some of the old monopolies, such as urban transport, were broken up under pressure from new participants, breaking down some of the old exclusive barriers. Some *cruceño* institutions, once run by elites for elites, found themselves opening up to these new participants. In rural areas too, some of those who migrated to the department as *colonizadores* had themselves become significant players within the agricultural complex, not least as *soyeros*.

Finally, the relationship between La Paz and Santa Cruz – which turned highly antagonistic in 2008 – may not be quite as conflictual as it is sometimes portrayed. That the economic elite has chosen to adopt a 'business' attitude towards the Morales administration, based more on pragmatism than on ideological considerations, appears to be a significant step. This has been reciprocated by the government, aware that Santa Cruz is the main source of food for the rest of the country. Policy towards agricultural producers (both large and small) – land, credit and marketing – has thus come to favour Santa Cruz. The extent to which this prejudices others in other parts of the country may turn out to be a source of fresh tensions. Thus the future of Santa Cruz promises to be significantly different to the past. The old patterns of control appear to be breaking down, its institutions are beginning to become more pluralist, and its politics rather more democratic in the way they operate. And a new relationship appears to be opening up between Santa Cruz and the rest of Bolivia, a rather less chauvinistic attitude based on a more inclusive sort of politics.

8 | THE AMAZONIAN NORTH

The department of Pando and the province of Vaca Diez in the department of the Beni (along with the province of Iturralde in the north of La Paz) together constitute a region of Bolivia that is unlike any other. The northern territories have, until recently, been largely cut off from the rest of the country. It was only at the beginning of the 1990s, with the construction of a road linking the towns of Cobija (the capital of Pando) and Riberalta (the provincial capital of Vaca Diez) with La Paz, that there was any sort of terrestrial link. The economy of the region has traditionally been more integrated with Brazil than the rest of Bolivia. According to Enrique Ormachea, from CEDLA, who worked in the region in the early 1980s, 'the only thing you could buy [at that time] that wasn't Brazilian was Bolivian beer'. The main products of the region – rubber and Brazil nuts – were shipped out down the Amazon river system to Manaus and Belém, and the main cultural influences were also Brazilian, notably television. But it has seen other cycles of boom and bust based on extractive industries: quinine (the cure for malaria) was an early contender, and more recently there have been the timber industry and the quest for alluvial gold in the region's majestic rivers.

This was therefore a remote place to which relatively few Bolivians ventured, far from the main axes of growth, a place with its own peculiar history. It is, however, one of the areas of the country that has undergone the most striking change over the last thirty years or so. This is a story of the development of extractive industries, particularly that of the Brazil nut, the introduction of important changes in traditional systems of land tenure, the development of new forms of social organization, the immigration of large numbers of people into a previously sparsely populated region, the emergence of new forms of economic activity, and finally the construction of state institutions.

On the frontier

What is now Pando and the north of the Beni was an inhospitable place, far from the centres of colonial prosperity, which straddled the boundaries of what were the Portuguese and Spanish spheres of influence. On colonial maps it was labelled *'tierra incognita'*, the unknown land. Though colonial pioneers had sought to penetrate the lush forests of Amazonia, it was never an easy enterprise, and voyages of exploration normally ended in frustration or disaster. Not even the Jesuits, those intrepid savers of souls of the colonial period who built churches and missionary settlements in the remote Chiquitanía and in much of the Beni, ventured this far into the Amazon jungle. Some of the indigenous peoples who inhabited this part of what was to become Bolivia were drawn into the local economy as cheap labour.

What drew the interest of outsiders to the region was the allure of a new commodity which was to create huge fortunes for those who exploited it across the jungles of Amazonia: rubber. The invention of the pneumatic tyre made rubber a hugely profitable product in the early years of the twentieth century, attracting businessmen and investors from across the world, but particularly from Europe. Huge fortunes were to be made, and boom towns sprang up in the Amazon in places where this valuable commodity was gathered and traded, such as Manaus in Brazil and Iquitos in Peru, both of which boasted flamboyant opera houses. Tapped from trees growing wild in the jungle, rubber was shipped down the rivers of Amazonia to towns built at points of confluence, where major rivers joined. In Bolivia, one such town was Riberalta, built at the point where the Beni joins the mighty Madre de Díos river. Founded in 1880, it was a point at which rubber from all over the Bolivian jungle could be gathered and stored, pending shipment downriver. A river boat that plied these rivers, the *Tahuamanu* – built in Annan, Scotland, and which entered service in 1899 – stands mounted on a concrete plinth on the riverside park in Riberalta as a memorial to the town's early days.

The 'king' of Bolivian rubber was Nicolás Suárez, and most of what was to become the department of Pando in 1938 was the territory of the Casa Suárez. Suárez built his headquarters downstream from Riberalta at a place called Cachuela Esperanza. This was a strategic location on the Madre de Díos at the point where a series of rapids separated the Bolivian river system from that of the lower Amazon; rubber had to be hauled round the rapids here before it could be shipped off downstream into Brazil. Suárez built a settlement at Cachuela Esperanza, founded in the 1880s. The town boasted ample housing, a theatre and Suárez's own mansion. Today what remains of Suárez's jungle capital is encroached upon by exuberant jungle vegetation. To circumvent the rapids, a railway was built along the Mamoré and Madeira rivers. Thousands died in the process from mosquito-borne diseases. According to Professor Herman González, a historian from Riberalta, each sleeper on the section between Guayaramerín and San Antonio supposedly represents a railway worker who died in the process of construction.

The rubber boom coincided with the loss by Bolivia of what was to become the state of Acre after a short conflict in 1902/03. In reality, this was a war not between nations but between rival rubber interests. A monument to their 'patriotism' is to be found in the centre of Cobija. Those who mobilized to 'defend' Bolivia were mainly indentured rubber tappers belonging to the Casa Suárez. In return for ceding Acre, Bolivia received an indemnity of £2 million from Brazil, which was largely used to construct the railways from Santa Cruz to Corumbá in Brazil and from La Paz to Antofagasta in Chile. The heyday of the rubber industry ended almost as abruptly as it began, following the transplantation of rubber plants from the Amazon to plantations in Malaya, where it could be produced more cheaply. The industry continued, however, albeit a shadow of its former self, until the beginning of the 1980s, when the removal of a subsidy paid in Brazil finally forced Bolivian rubber traders out of business. Many of those who had been employed as rubber tappers – often in situations of indentured labour – were obliged to migrate to towns like Riberalta. For its part, the Casa Suárez collapsed in 1952, at the time of the Bolivian revolution.

Rubber ended up being replaced by the Brazil nut (*castaña* or *almendra*) in the local economy. The traditional system of landholding, the *barraca*, in which both rubber and Brazil nuts were extracted from the native jungle, collapsed with the demise of the rubber industry. *Barracas* covered huge extensions of land. The Casa Suárez had laid claim to more than a million hectares of land. Following its fall, most *barraqueros* were far less powerful figures, although their holdings were often extremely large. Many migrated to the towns, where they formed the basis of the local administration. The traditional system of landholding was already in decay well before new laws were passed in the 1990s to regulate landownership in the eastern lowlands. Those who continued to work in the *barracas* were peasants who dedicated themselves to the collection of Brazil nuts, the only source of income in much of Bolivian Amazonia following the final collapse of the rubber industry. The system of employment in the *barracas* was typically one where the *patrón* wielded almost complete authority over a workforce for whom labour rights were unknown.

Brazil nuts

Riberalta is today the world capital of the perhaps inappropriately named Brazil nut. Whereas in past decades Brazil was the main producer and Peru the runner-up, Bolivia has been producing around 70 per cent of the world supply of the nut since the late 1990s. According to Erlan Gamarra at the Empresa Boliviana de Almendra y Derivados (EBA), the newly established state trading company, brokers from around the world come to Riberalta to do their business. In 2011, total production in Bolivia reached around 200,000 tons. In 1975, Brazil was by far the largest producer with a total output of 80,000 tons. Bolivia at the time accounted for only 20 per cent of world supply.

Not only has production increased a great deal in Bolivia since the collapse of rubber, but the nature of the business has changed radically. Until the construction of the road linking Riberalta and La Paz, all of Bolivia's nut production was exported downriver to Manaus, where the nuts were processed and packaged for export to Europe and North America. Today, all of Bolivia's production is processed locally and exported to the world market through La Paz and the ports of northern Chile. Although the way that Brazil nuts are grown has not changed – they come from huge trees growing wild in the rainforest – the 1980s saw the development in Bolivia of the processing industry, a form of factory production. Of the twenty factories, most are located in Riberalta; there are three in

Cobija and one in Puerto Rico (both in the department of Pando). Some of these plants are highly mechanized. The Tahuamanu factory in Cobija is probably the most sophisticated in South America, though most of the factories in Riberalta use more rudimentary production methods and machinery. About 70 per cent of Bolivia's production goes to the European market; most of the remainder is bought by the United States. The first consignment of Brazil nuts was sent to China in 2011.

Prices for Brazil nuts were buoyant up until 2011, though traders in Riberalta foresaw a downturn in 2012, reflecting a drop in European demand. In the 1990s, a case of 20 kilograms would fetch around 40 bolivianos, while in 2012, at the time of writing, a case cost 250 bolivianos. While demand had increased substantially, supply remained roughly the same. Although the economy of Riberalta, and indeed the whole Amazonian north, remained perilously dependent on this one product, the rise in prices brought clear benefits to the population of the region. In terms of numbers, there are around 10,000 families whose livelihoods depend directly on the production of *castaña*, mostly peasant producers working in the jungle, but also some *barraqueros* too. But another 15,000 families are involved in the annual harvesting of the nut, a further 5,000 working in factories, making a total of 30,000 families. The harvest takes place between December and March, and the income it generates has to last for much of the rest of the year. In fact, it does not do so, and families who work the *zafra* (harvest) and have no other major source of income tend to end up in debt. The Brazil nut is the only nut in the world that is grown in the wild, not in plantations. According to Gamarra at EBA, you can produce 5 tons of macadamia nuts per hectare each year, whereas you get only around 20 kilos per hectare of Brazil nuts. The advantage of Brazil nuts, of course, is that they help maintain the integrity of the jungle. However, 'consumers in Europe don't realize that they are helping to care for the forest', says Marcelo Sapiencia, also at EBA. Because of the traditional methods used, some producers gain a premium for their output for producing organic and respecting Fair Trade principles.

Partly because of the buoyancy of the Brazil nut market, incomes in this part of Bolivia tend to be higher than elsewhere. CIPCA, the national rural promotion NGO which conducts an annual survey of incomes in the areas where it operates, estimates that peasants in Pando and Vaca Diez earn more than anywhere else in Bolivia, a total of around 30,000 bolivianos (about US$4,000) a year. Still, poverty remains quite widespread, and the system of debt bondage, known as '*habilito*', continues to work in practice in many places, with intermediaries facilitating goods to the harvest workers (*zafreros*) before they are able to pay it back. According to Marcos Nordgren, the director of CIPCA in Riberalta, a short-term mentality prevails, with little saving. 'Money there is,' he says, 'but it does not translate into welfare.' For most people, the money earned from the harvest runs out by the following July, and the remaining months of the year are extremely hard. This is also partly to do with the behaviour of local salesmen, who raise what they charge for food and other consumer items during the high season of nut collection when people have more money in their pockets.

The benefits of higher prices for *castaña* in recent years have tended to accrue mainly to the peasant population and the *recolectores* (harvesters). Those working in the processing plants have not done so well. Employment in the factories of Riberalta and Cobija is pre-eminently female. Of the 14,000–15,000 workers employed in the region, between 60 and 70 per cent are women. The work they do – mostly in the breaking up of the nuts (*quebrada*) and their selection into grades – is paid by the amount they produce, with one woman usually producing a bag of 18–20 kilograms a day, more if they involve members of their family. Most women expect to earn 50–200 bolivianos a day, beginning work at 5 a.m. when the temperatures are coolest. But most of the processing plants (*beneficiadoras*) do not work the whole year, and the employees have to find alternative occupations during the idle months. Only in the largest factories – Urkupiña in Riberalta and Tahuamanu in Cobija – do they work throughout the year; these are the most mechanized, where many jobs have been replaced by machines. According to Limberth Siriora, a union leader in Riberalta who worked previously in Tahuamanu, 'with the introduction of machinery seventy per cent of the workers lost their jobs'.

Most of the *castaña* that is produced comes from the jungle area in Pando, especially in the eastern areas closer to Riberalta. This is where the jungle is still largely intact. As you fly from Riberalta to Cobija, the so-called 'green carpet' below you becomes increasingly threadbare as you approach Cobija. This is where the process of deforestation is clearest, where as a result of slash and burn activities the land has been turned over to livestock. In the jungle, however, production of *castaña* takes place on large extensions of land, since the number of trees per hectare is normally no more than two or three.

The purpose of EBA is to try to increase the returns to those harvesting *castaña* by improving the amount of information available to producers. It publishes a bulletin every two months in order to make the business more transparent. Although EBA buys *castaña*, it purchases from only a small part of the market. Rather it seeks to create links with the *recolectores*, and to help them negotiate better market prices for their produce. 'Everyone wants more from the cake, but last year [2011], the producers got a much bigger slice,' says Erlan Gamarra. The organization, set up in 2007, buys about 40 per cent of the Brazil nuts it handles from peasant and indigenous producers, and the rest from *barraqueros* and firms working on forestry concessions. According to Marcos Nordgren at CIPCA, 'EBA has had an impact, helping to raise prices and forcing other buyers to improve what they pay [...] but it remains to be seen if these increases are sustainable'. Rosa Quete, a former campesina leader in Riberalta, is less complimentary. EBA 'is just another company', she says. 'It should be producing other benefits for the people here.'

Saneamiento and land titling

While the changes that took place in the Amazonian north in the 1980s and 1990s were, to a large extent, a result of changes in market conditions and the construction of the road to the rest of Bolivia, the process of *saneamiento* and land titling – first ushered in under the 1996 INRA land legislation, but greatly accelerated under the Morales government – has had a profound effect on the nature of production and its social effects. At the time of writing, Pando was the only department in Bolivia where the process of *saneamiento* (with the exception of a handful of communities) was complete.

According to official figures from the INRA, a total of 3.7 million hectares of *tierras fiscales* were identified between 2006 and 2010 in the department of Pando alone. Of this total, a large part has been awarded to peasant and indigenous communities principally working the *castaña* harvest.

The areas awarded are large, given the nature of *castaña* production and the vulnerability of tropical soils ill suited for agriculture. Land is held collectively among communities and cannot be sold to others, the idea being to avoid subdivision of the land and a return to the excessive land concentration of the past. However, within communities, individual families have been awarded, on average, around five hundred hectares each. There is some variation in this, giving rise to criticism. According to Manuel Lima, a former general secretary of the peasant federation in Pando, some families were awarded considerably more than this, which he called 'a crime'. But as Rosa Quete pointed out to us, the number of *castaña* trees also varies a lot. She claimed to have 320 trees on her land in the community of Santa María, forty-five minutes from Riberalta. Others, she says, have 'barely twenty trees'. Besides *castaña* collection, people also have access to timber, rubber, hunting and fishing.

The process of land titling has had the effect of drastically changing the traditional patterns of land tenure. Although the old *barracas* had mostly disappeared by the 1980s, *saneamiento* led to a substantial reduction in the amount of land held by private individuals who lacked formal land titles and failed to comply with strictures about productive use. In some cases, we were told, *barraqueros* had been reduced to holding only relatively small plots of 50 hectares. The old system of landholding under which a handful of families dominated the local economy and society thus finally disappeared. According to Juan Fernando Reyes of the NGO Herencia in Cobija, as a consequence of *titulación*, peasants and indigenous peoples hold about 40 per cent of the land in the department of Pando, while around 10 per cent remains in private hands and 30 per cent is held in the form of forestry concessions from the state (without any title of ownership but where those holding concessions enjoy the right to exploit resources on them). Among those who lost land were Brazilian settlers who found it difficult to justify their presence.

Land titling and *saneamiento* appear to have been achieved reasonably harmoniously in the Amazon region, helping to explain how such large areas of land were allocated in a relatively short period of time. In part, this is due to the fact that 'there is enough land [here] for everyone', says Marcos Nordgren at CIPCA. However, for those most closely involved, it was not achieved without significant pressure and against opposition from elite groups. 'The establishment of TCOs was very important [to us],' says Edgar Amutari, 'but it was we who gave impetus to the process of change.' Amutari, who belongs to the Takana people in the region of Santa Rosa, is the secretary for land and territory at Cirabo, the Central Indígena de la Región Amazónica de Bolivia. For his part, Calixto Cartagena, a member of the Caviñeno people (who also form part of Cirabo), told us how the only way to gain land was through mobilization. 'The government made us see that the only way to achieve things is through direct pressure [...] all the legislation has been a consequence of pressure from below.' According to Manuel Lima, the process of land distribution had to contend with opposition from those with forestry concessions, *barraqueros* and conservative politicians who have long held sway in Pando.

However, one of the chief concerns of those working with peasant organizations in the region is the utilization of the land that has been distributed as a consequence of land titling. 'There are communities with thousands of hectares, but which lack the ability to transform landowning into income,' says Marcos Nordgren; 'this opens the way for land piracy' with the intrusion of outsiders keen to make a quick buck out of exploiting timber resources or burning the forest and turning it over to pasture for cattle rearing. Government policies seen as encouraging the extension of the agricultural frontier came in for a good deal of criticism from those we talked to, particularly those working with indigenous groups and protecting the environment. There has been relatively little assistance made available to peasants and indigenous groups to invest in activities like eco-tourism and the cultivation of wild cocoa that raise income without destroying the forest cover. At the same time, outside Pando, *saneamiento* and land titling still have a long way to go. In Beni, for example, 'it's far from complete and there is still much [land] to *sanear*', Nordgren says.

But the process of land titling in the Amazon region appears to be an irreversible change that has brought both economic and social stability and security to a large portion of the population which, in previous generations, had been one of the most exploited anywhere in Bolivia. Monsignor Luis Casey, who hails from St Louis in the United States and has been bishop of Riberalta since the mid-1980s, has witnessed changes there at first hand. He says, 'one of the best things, and I am proud to say it, is that organization has led to campesinos gaining title to the land', a process in which the Catholic Church, alongside NGOs and peasant *sindicatos*, has been closely involved. In particular he applauds the legalization of land by community rather than by individual ownership. 'This keeps communities together,' he says.

Social organization

Given the traditional structures of landownership bequeathed from the time of rubber extraction, social organization in the region is weak compared to other parts of Bolivia. Labour relations in the *barracas* were paternalistic at best, downright repressive at worst. It was not an environment conducive to organization. As César Aguilar, a historian from Cobija, puts it, 'in Pando there is not much of a tradition of communal organization [...] but with the fragmentation of the *barracas*, there was greater space in which workers could begin to organize'. The panorama has changed in important ways over the last twenty years, reflecting both structural changes in the nature of the local economy as well as the influence of outsiders – the Catholic Church, NGOs and (not least) the state.

As in other parts of the eastern lowlands of Bolivia, indigenous organization has developed in defence of land and other rights. As elsewhere, the notion of rights and the demand for these to be included in the constitution were key elements of an emerging political participation that stemmed originally from the formation of the Confederación de Pueblos Indígenas de Bolivia (Cidob) and the 1990 march from Trinidad to La Paz. The formation of the Cirabo, whose headquarters is in Riberalta, was a key development in terms of collaboration between indigenous organizations in the region. The Cirabo includes the Chácobo, the Cavineño, the Takana, the Esse Ejja, the Araona, the Pacahuara and the Joaquiniano peoples. Several of these are relatively small in number, occupying very large extensions of land as TCOs. According to Mónica Lijerón from CEJIS in Riberalta, an NGO which prioritizes work with indigenous groups, the peoples who make up the Cirabo were awarded 1.7 million hectares in the region. However, according to Guillermo Rioja, an anthropologist who works in the university in Cobija, the number of tribes that can be truly described as 'indigenous' in the region, such as the Yaminawa and the Machineri, is fairly small. 'People like the Takana are no longer really indigenous tribes; they are thoroughly accultured in the anthropological sense [...] although the Esse-Ejja are a little more closed off,' he says. However, whether accultured or not, indigenous groups have actively pursued the objective of having their lands and their rights recognized officially. 'Only fairly recently have we managed to secure land title,' says Calixto Cartagena of the Cavineño people, 'and this was a great achievement for us.'

Peasants in Pando and Vaca Diez are far more numerous than the members of indigenous groupings, many of them former workers for the *barraqueros* (at least those of them who did not migrate to the towns when the bottom finally fell out of the rubber industry). Unlike the indigenous peoples, they have a stronger tradition of working as labourers in the *barracas* and have only recently begun to develop a sense of community. Most peasants have their own small plot of agricultural land on which they grow crops like yuca, rice and maize, and are more integrated into the market economy. In some cases, they include former members of indigenous tribes, like the Takana, who were drawn into work on the rubber estates. Indeed, unlike in some other parts of Bolivia, relations between peasant and indigenous organizations have recently been harmonious; this is probably due to the fact that they are both involved in the same economic activity and have faced a common opponent, the *barraquero*. The Bloque de Organizaciones Campesinas e Indígenas del Norte Amazónico de Bolivia (BOCINAB) has provided a joint platform and, in Marcos Nordgren's words, 'a space for ideas and proposals to emerge'. He adds that 'land has been a factor of unity here'.

Like indigenous groups, the peasant federations of the region played an active role in pressing for land titling from as early on as

2001. Empowered by the upsurge of social movements in the years that followed, the Pando Peasant Federation managed to achieve important advances. According to Manuel Lima, the federation's former leader, 140 communities received title to the land between 2006 and 2007. However, peasant organization in Pando proved difficult to sustain, particularly with Leopoldo Fernández as prefect of the department. Fernández, who belonged to Banzer's Acción Democrática Nacionalista (ADN) party, proved adept at co-opting leaders with promises of small-scale development schemes in the communities of the department. He tended to act in a paternalistic fashion, making decisions for those around him, rather like the head of a *barraca*. His main allies were among the cattle rearers and timber extractors of the department.

Parallel to the development of peasant organization, there has been significant development among women campesinas under the aegis of the Federación de Mujeres Campesinas Bartolina Sisa, both in Pando and in Riberalta. Here again, there has been a flourishing of concepts of rights, both of women as producers within the peasant community and as partners within the household. Closely allied to the MAS, the Bartolinas have certainly made their mark, even in Pando, where machismo still prevails in both public and private life. At a meeting of Bartolinas in Riberalta, we were left in no doubt as to the determination of the women present. 'We were marginalized, but now our rights are included in the constitution, so now we have to be respected,' says Gladys Eamara; 'we want rights to the land as women.' One of the advances included in the land titling programme of recent years has been the inclusion of both women and men as registered owners of their land. 'But this is definitely not the rule in our community,' Gladys adds. The women we met were appreciative of the social changes that had come about in recent years. 'They're going to build a big hospital [here] in Riberalta,' says Kendy Cortés, with babe in arms; 'there are also the *bonos*, the Bono Juancito Pinto, the Juana Azurduy.' But life as a leader of the Bartolinas is not easy, and some of those we spoke to were separated from their husbands, partly because of their activities beyond the household. The problems facing women *dirigentes* were echoed too by Adisol Chávez, executive secretary of the Bartolinas in Pando. 'We are beginning to make demands, urban and rural communities together,' she says. She recounted how, together with women colleagues, they walked out of a meeting of the campesino federation because the men would not accept them as possible leaders.

Social organization is notably stronger among the workers of the processing plants in Riberalta, affiliated at the national level to the manufacturing workers' union, the Confederación de Fabriles. Because of the nature of the workforce in the *beneficiadoras*, most of the members of the local branch of *fabriles* are women, though its main leader is a man, Limberth Siriora. According to Limberth, significant advances have been made in recent years, such as payment for Sunday working and time off for nursing mothers. He and his fellow leaders talked with enthusiasm about the changes which they have helped bring about. Each worker contributes three bolivianos per week to the union, of which one goes to the federation, one to the *sindicato*, and one to pay for a full-time lawyer to provide legal back-up in industrial disputes. The federation intervenes in the various processing plants to ensure that labour standards are maintained. But even in this 'proletarian' world (to borrow Enrique Ormachea's phrase), union activity is not easy. Limberth was threatened by management at Urkupiña where he worked, and was eventually sacked for his work with the union. He spent ten months without pay. 'The problem is that here union rights are not respected,' he says. The union, for example, has been unable to prevent workers being dismissed where factories undergo mechanization.

Finally, at the urban level, there is social organization within each neighbourhood through the *juntas vecinales*. The towns of both Riberalta and Cobija have grown exponentially in recent years. Precise numbers for both are hard to come by, but Riberalta, which had a population of 43,000 at the time of the 1992 census, now has one of around 130,000. It has attracted a significant amount of migration, both from rural areas near by and from other departments. Cobija is much the same. According to the 1992 census, it had a population of 10,000. In 2012, according to the mayoress, Ana Lucia Reis, it was in the region of 100,000, with a huge influx of migrants both from the Altiplano and from other parts of eastern Bolivia. New neighbourhoods have grown up almost overnight in both towns, and with them neighbourhood organizations with the express purpose of achieving basic services like water, electricity and sewerage. 'It's growing far too rapidly, and in a very chaotic way,' says Ana Lucia Reis, Cobija's first MAS mayor. The most recent neighbourhoods in Cobija, located on squatted land beyond the airport, include Perla de Acre, 6 de Enero and 6 de Agosto. Darwin Araujo, who is a local *dirigente* of the *junta vecinal* in Madre de Nazaria, recalls how they lacked paved streets and drinking water:

> Previously you had to walk to the community well to get water, and in the rainy season it was almost impossible to enter the community for all the mud [...] now, social movements can express our needs; previously we were unable to get a hearing [...] We now have the telephone number of the mayoress.

Darwin highlighted the fact that there was also street lighting, paving and the construction of a school costing 5 million bolivianos. 'The advances made since 2006 have been very significant,' he concludes, though he admits that the work of the *juntas* is impeded by internal political differences.

Emporium of the north

The town of Cobija is built on a large bend in the River Acre, surrounded by Brazil on three sides, with access to the town of Brasilea across the 'Bridge of Fraternity'. First established in 1906, until the 1960s it was a sleepy town of a few hundred people whose main street consisted of brightly painted wooden buildings, along which ox-carts were the main form of vehicular traction. Today, the same street is of large (rather ugly) concrete buildings housing emporia selling all manner of electric and other luxury goods to largely Brazilian customers. Cobija is the only departmental capital in Bolivia situated on a frontier. And since it is the frontier between one of Latin America's most expensive countries and one of its cheapest, it naturally favours the flow of commerce. And since the revaluation of the Brazilian real in 2005, it has become the target for Brazilian bargain hunters, who flood across the Bridge of Fraternity each day (but particularly at weekends) to do their shopping and return home with their cars laden up to the roof.

To encourage foreign trade, private investment and industrial development, Cobija was made a free port (*zona franca*) in 1983. But what it has seen since then is commercial not industrial development. Because of the high cost of electricity and the lack of good roads linking it with the rest of Bolivia, few industries have set themselves up in the town. The exception is the Tahuamanu factory, one of the largest processors of *castaña*. Otherwise, and apart from the *zona franca*, the main source of employment is small-scale enterprises, mostly in the informal sector. Given the importance of the *zona franca* to the generation of wealth, the town's status as such has now been extended to 2018. The fact that it is tax free – and taxes are high in Brazil – means that the *zona franca* has also attracted high-powered Brazilian traders, who sell smart clothes, designer watches, fine wines and whisky in volumes not seen in most other parts of the world. They represent global brand names. According to Ana Lucia Reis, one particularly large store in Cobija has a turnover of US$61 million a year. All in all, the town is a bubble far removed from the rest of Pando.

Two other developments have helped shape the growth of Cobija into what a Brazilian magazine has recently called '*o Miami do Acre*'. One was the building of the road to La Paz. Though impassable during much of the rainy season, the road provides the means by which goods flow into Cobija from the outside world. Many of these are contraband items made in China, and then shipped into Bolivia through the port of Iquique. For Brazilians, it is far cheaper to buy Chinese-made refrigerators, electronic devices and a myriad of other gadgets in Cobija than in Rio Branco, the capital of Acre. With a number of road-building schemes going on in and around Cobija, the city is no longer cut off from the rest of the world. 'Whereas all rivers used to lead to Riberalta, now all roads lead to Cobija,' says Guillermo Rioja of the Universidad Amazónica de Pando.

The second is the massive migration into Cobija from other parts of Bolivia, but particularly from the Altiplano. With their zest for commercial activity, it is largely people from the '*kolla*' community who work the markets and emporia of Cobija. Most of them are young, arrive poor but quickly find ways of improving their condition, buying and selling or providing other services such as urban transport. A good deal of the money earned in Cobija returns to the families of migrants in La Paz, Oruro and Cochabamba.

Migrants from the Altiplano thus contribute to the cultural mix that is Cobija. They bring with them their taste for music and dance, their traditions of ample clothing for women (despite the intense heat of Pando), and their practices of social organization. The *sindicato* of motorcycle taxi drivers, for instance, is an import from cities like El Alto. But not all those who have flocked to Cobija come from the highlands. There are many migrants too from the Beni, Santa Cruz and from within Pando itself. As in Riberalta, the collapse of the rubber industry in Pando encouraged former campesinos to flock to the towns in search of alternative employment. According to Darwin Araujo, more than half the migrants in his neighbourhood came from the Beni. He himself was born in Guayaramerín, and his father used to navigate the River Mamoré in the days of rubber extraction. Apart from working as a motorcycle taxi driver and as leader of his local *junta vecinal*, Darwin sells watches, mobile phones and baseball caps, which he buys wholesale in the markets of La Paz and Santa Cruz.

As well as being a commercial throughput, the town is also a conduit for other forms of contraband. Since the retail price of petrol in Bolivia is a fraction of what it is in Brazil, there is a lively trade in fuel going across the frontier. Brazilian motorists also come to Cobija not just to buy consumer goods but to fill up their tanks. Drug trafficking is also in evidence in the town and along Pando's border with Peru (almost impossible to control) and also that with Brazil.

Presence of the state

No longer is it the case that the Amazonian north is cut off from the rest of Bolivia, gravitating more towards Brazil than anywhere else. Nor is it the case that the state is conspicuous by its absence. 'Before, there was no presence of the state here,' says Mónica Lijerón at CEJIS in Riberalta, 'and a few families controlled everything.' Most of those we interviewed reiterated this point, but not all agreed that this was necessarily a good thing.

The presence of state institutions has been growing over the last quarter-century. According to César Aguilar, the Cobija historian, this incremental expansion received a particular boost under the government of Jaime Paz Zamora (1989–93) when local politicians – many linked to Hugo Banzer's right-wing ADN – gained considerable influence in government. However, state presence has increased dramatically since the Morales government took office in 2006. There are two key reasons for this.

The first is the introduction of the new tax on hydrocarbons (IDH), introduced in 2006. This provided Pando with large amounts of cash, both to pay the local administration but also to increase public investment. Under the formula chosen for distribution of the IDH, 30 per cent of the proceeds are divided up equally between Bolivia's nine departments. Because of Pando's relatively small population – tides of migration notwithstanding – it has been a disproportionate beneficiary of the IDH. 'The flow of resources got going in 2006 and 2007,' says Carol Carlo, a sociologist at the Universidad Amazónica in Cobija; 'this has been channelled through the municipality, the governor's office and the university.' She points out of her window at the flurry of building work going on on the university campus. 'This has had a very dynamic effect on the local economy, through its multiplier effects,' she says. According to Ana Lucia Reis, public investment in Cobija has grown by 70 per cent, due mainly to IDH. 'We are spending much more now on education,' she says. Because of the tax exemptions in the city, only a tiny fraction of the municipal budget – a mere 3.5–4 per cent – comes from local taxes.

The second major factor is more political in nature. In September 2008, a number of peasants were shot and killed at the township of Porvenir, near Cobija, in what has become known since as the 'Pando massacre'. Accounts vary a good deal as to what actually happened but, as a result of the killings, the then prefect of Pando, Leopoldo Fernández, was arrested and imprisoned for his alleged responsibility. Several of the people we spoke to said that he was the person behind what took place. For the MAS government in La Paz, the Pando killings – which took place at the same time as and were seemingly inspired by the riots that took place in Santa Cruz, Tarija and other spots in the *media luna* – were a red alert. In 2010 Evo Morales decided that Juan Ramón Quintana, the minister of the presidency from 2006 to 2009 and a key member of his entourage, should be made head of a new organization (Ademaf) charged with state development in frontier areas, including Pando. A controversial figure, he has played a key role in building up state institutions in the Amazonian north. According to Mónica Lijerón from CEJIS, 'the government has paid attention to the region, with a greater presence of *oficialismo*, of the ministries, of the municipalities', particularly in Riberalta, where a MAS mayor was elected for the first time in 2010. The same pattern is observable in Cobija, where Ana Lucia Reis was the first ever successful MAS candidate in elections there.

Other signs of an increased state presence in the region include the creation of organizations like EBA (the Empresa Boliviana de Almendras) and EBO (the Empresa Boliviana del Oro). EBO has the task of overseeing the production of alluvial gold in the rivers of the north and ensuring that production is channelled through the state, in particular the central bank. 'For the first time people realize that the government has some concern for the region,' says Erlan Gamarra at EBA; 'we are part of that concern for state building.'

But not everyone shares this enthusiasm for the expansion of the state. For some, like Guillermo Rioja, the idea of developing the frontier stems from a preoccupation with building the state from the centre outwards, a preoccupation with a long history going back to the times of the MNR. He belongs to a group known as MAP (Madre de Dios, Acre, Pando) which seeks to promote a multi-national approach based on the common interests and history of the Amazonian region. 'This sort of relationship does not exist elsewhere in Bolivia,' he says, 'and does not square with the centralizing, state-building mentality in La Paz.' Juan Fernando Reyes, at Herencia, is also a proponent of the MAP project. He too stresses the specific ecological characteristics of the region, and the differences that separate it from other parts of the Bolivian lowlands, particularly Santa Cruz. Manuel Lima, for his part, talks of the global importance of the region as a source of water for the future.

Many of those working in NGOs in the region, especially those working with peasants and indigenous groups, are also highly critical of the activities of the government – Quintana in particular – since 2008. They point to a growing modus vivendi between the state and traditional landowning interest groups in the region. Marcos Nordgren at CIPCA suggests that local elites, particularly since 2008, have seen which way the wind is blowing and have sought to do deals with the state. 'What I see is that they [the elites] have been astute and aligned themselves with the *proceso*,' he says, pointing to various instances in the region where members of old landowning families are exercising public functions in local administrations ostensibly led by the MAS. Mónica Lijerón is more trenchant in the language she uses: 'today, the government has allied itself with the local power groups and business people'. Many of those involved in social organizations are critical too. Manuel Lima, former leader of the peasant federation in Pando, for instance, sees the Morales administration carrying on many of the clientelistic practices which had helped sustain Fernández in office until his fall from grace in 2008. For his part, Edgar Amutari, from the Takana indigenous people, is damning in his critique of government policies: 'the government is [now] working against the indigenous peoples', he says.

Conclusions

The Amazonian north is perhaps one of the regions of Bolivia which has undergone the most dramatic changes in recent decades. Cut off from the rest of the country, and with its own economic dynamic based first on rubber, then on *castaña*, it is a region where previously society was dominated by a small landed class that controlled vast areas of land. However, unlike other regions – such as Santa Cruz – it was an area where the main forms of production were based on the exploitation of the forest, not its destruction. The decline of the *barraqueros*, the impact of urbanization and the emergence of new social forces – particularly among the indigenous and peasant populations – have had transformative effects on both politics and society.

These changes are the result of both long-term trends and policy decisions by government. The *castaña* industry has proved one of Bolivia's unsung success stories. Traditionally controlled by Brazil, it has turned into an important export product that has gone from strength to strength in recent years. The *castaña* processing industry provides productive employment for thousands of urban workers, mainly women. The construction of roads that link the region with the rest of the country for the first time has changed the patterns of trade and marketing. Meanwhile, the demands for *saneamiento* and land titling from social organizations which were finally met by the Morales administration have led to a major shift in the structure of landholding in favour of the peasant (and indigenous) population. There have also been important changes at the level of popular organization. Traditionally a society where elites managed to maintain control through clientelistic and paternalistic relations with their workforce, it is now experiencing incipient organization in both the rural and urban areas. Urban areas have seen the development of both union activity, particularly in the *castaña* processing plants, and among the barrios of vastly expanded towns like Riberalta and Cobija. In rural areas, indigenous organizations and peasant *sindicatos* have proliferated. Unlike in other parts of Bolivia, they have done so fairly harmoniously, producing similar products, confronting similar adversaries and sharing common attitudes towards the land and landholding.

At the political level, the old elites have seen their power reduced. To a certain extent this pre-dated the advent of the MAS, as landowners withdrew from the *castaña* industry into bureaucratic activities within the local administration. However, the process of change has accelerated since 2006, and in particular since the removal of Leopoldo Fernández as prefect of Pando in 2008. The victory of the MAS in the 2010 municipal elections in towns such as Riberalta and Cobija represented a significant shift, even though landowning interests may have sought to find accommodation with the MAS. The state has made an effort to invest in the area, especially in social and physical infrastructure.

The region is no longer dominated in the way it used to be by Brazilian commerce and culture. It has become far more integrated with the rest of Bolivia because of the construction of road links, and has seen a much more tangible presence of state structures and authorities. These have brought thousands of migrants from the highlands, and with them commercial and cultural influences that are transforming places like Cobija, now an unlikely entrepôt between China and Brazil. The influence of the rest of Bolivia is in evidence: in Riberalta, we witnessed schoolchildren dancing *caporales* and *morenadas* in the main square, dances typical of the highlands.

And in addition to changing lifestyles, incomes are in the ascendant. The proliferation of motorcycles is one indicator; the local dealers for Honda and Suzuki must look on with satisfaction as they observe the sheer number of motorbikes that buzz around the main square of Riberalta like mosquitoes on a hot tropical night.

9 | CONCLUSIONS

This book has mapped out areas of change in Bolivia, particularly since 2006 when the Morales government first took office. It has highlighted people's perceptions of those changes, particularly those who have been actors in the 'process of change' in its various manifestations in different parts of the country. That there have been major changes there is little doubt, but their nature and intensity have been conditioned by their specific contexts. Arguably, taken as a whole, these processes of change have been the most significant since those that came about in the early 1950s as a result of the national revolution. The election of an indigenous person as president, particularly one from an impoverished background like Evo's, was important in itself, but it was a symbol of a much greater change taking place. The barriers that prevented people from a certain social extraction from reaching positions of power and influence had been effectively breached. It was, in part, this realization which imbued the Morales government with such significance for those who – by virtue of their class, ethnicity or gender – had found themselves excluded from the political and economic elites that traditionally ran the country. It was primarily for this reason that Evo's election as president created such expectations of change, expectations that proved difficult to meet in practice.

Many of the changes we have alluded to were the consequence of deep-rooted, long-term trends that had been in gestation for decades, if not generations. This book has stressed the changing economic and social contexts in which these trends emerged. The development of social movements had been a product of the political and social transformations that had themselves taken place over many years, but particularly in the 1990s and the first years of the new millennium when these movements emerged as forceful political actors both locally and nationally. They were the consequence, in part, of processes of urbanization and education which had gathered pace over decades. They were also a response to the liberalizing economic reforms of the 1980s and 1990s, and people's anger at the results. Finally, they were the result of the eventual breakdown of a political system of 'pacted democracy', a system of elite domination that had failed to cater for the needs and aspirations of large sectors of the population, and which contributed to institutional breakdown in the period before 2006.

The change in government in this year provided not only a change in regime but a new and more propitious context in which further changes could take place to deepen and institutionalize some of the transformations under way. While the agenda had been established back in October 2003, the 2005 elections brought to power a government committed to the implementation of that agenda. The reforms undertaken by the new government, and in particular the rewriting of the constitution, in themselves provided an impetus for further changes to take place. But they built on the earlier empowerment of previously excluded populations, creating new channels through which they could express themselves. The election of Evo Morales helped give these empowered social movements a voice in the processes of government, a voice they had never had before.

It thus seems improbable that, even if the Morales government fails to meet the expectations vested in it, and when the MAS is eventually supplanted, there will be a return to the status quo ante. New political actors have emerged in public life that will not easily be displaced. They include peasants, indigenous peoples and members of the *juntas vecinales* of the cities. They also include women; one of the notable features of popular organization in contemporary Bolivia is the presence of women at all levels, in ways unimaginable in the relatively recent past. The processes of change have opened up channels for women's participation in a host of different contexts. Old *machista* politics, it seems fair to say, are a thing of the past, though this is not to say that machismo has disappeared; far from it. As the women we interviewed attested, opening spaces for women's involvement has not been without a struggle and not without personal cost.

We have also seen how, in a variety of different geographical contexts, new economic actors have come to the fore, creating new forms of economic activity and (in some cases) rivalling and even displacing traditional forms of production and those involved. They include Aymara entrepreneurs in El Alto, quinua farmers on the Altiplano, former *colonizadores* in Santa Cruz, now prosperous *soyeros*, peasant farmers in Tarija, and those involved in mining cooperatives that have benefited from several years of buoyant mineral prices. By the same token, old elites have been marginalized or supplanted, or at least their ability to protect their interests has been challenged. We have seen examples of this with the decline of the old oligarchy in Tarija, the virtual elimination of the *barraqueros* in the north of the country, and the declining influence of political elites in Santa Cruz and of those institutions that have long protected their interests. The last of these may prove to be one of the key changes brought about during this period.

A more complex, inclusive and participatory society therefore seems to be in gestation, in which some of the old social (and racial) divides appear to be breaking down and a more pluralistic and democratic society emerging in which the old exclusions are a thing of the past. This is, of course, not to say that this is not a society in which there are many who remain mired in poverty and in which deep inequalities persist. But it is a society in which those from poor backgrounds are no longer blocked from reaching positions of power and authority; a society in which indigenous peoples are no longer denied access to public places; a society in which slavery is no longer tolerated; and a society in which women dressed in *polleras* can become deputies and senators or occupy ministerial roles.

The importance of the new constitution in this 'new' Bolivia is something that was widely commented upon by those we interviewed. It was seen as a major victory by those who had long pushed for a Constituent Assembly as a means to secure changes in the longer term. It was seen as an important 'learning curve' by those personally involved in the elaboration of the constitution with all the conflicts it entailed, an experience that turned *protesta* into *propuesta* (protest into proposal). And even though some of its sections were watered down at the last minute in political negotiations, its provisions – especially with regard to indigenous and women's rights – were widely seen as path-breaking. Although not all its articles were new (many were derived from previous constitutions), the Constituent

Assembly was not just an exercise in mild constitutional amendment; it represented an important break with the institutional architecture of the past, not least in terms of respect for indigenous rights.

However, turning a document such as this into a legally binding framework of rights and responsibilities was always likely to be complex, conflictive and time consuming. While winning an absolute majority of seats in the new Plurinational Legislative Assembly was clearly an advantage – helping to avoid the sort of horse-trading that had characterized passage of the constitution prior to 2009 – translating constitutional provisions into detailed legislation was not to be without its own political problems. In many respects, approval of the constitution was just the end of the beginning. In the years that followed the ratification of the constitution, it became ever clearer that there were many areas where the constitution had failed to resolve key areas of difficulty and disagreement. The consensus which had emerged with the ratification of the constitution would prove hard to sustain. At the same time, new sorts of problems emerged, creating sharp dilemmas for those in control of state decision-making.

Building a 'plurinational state' would prove harder in practice than on paper. The idea of a state composed of thirty-six 'nations' was an important statement of support for indigenous peoples and their autonomy to run their affairs in line with time-honoured *usos y costumbres*. But it was less clear how this would operate in practice and what it would mean for other sectors of society to which this sort of communitarian tradition was unfamiliar, not least in a context of rapid urbanization. The constitution envisaged special representation for indigenous peoples, but rather than there being representatives of the various different 'nations' in the new legislative assembly, this representation was eventually whittled down to just seven seats reserved for indigenous peoples. The extent to which they would be granted autonomy to manage their affairs would also not be without problems, particularly where such autonomy clashed with other priorities of the state – as in the development of gas fields. The creation of a dual justice system, with traditional forms of justice prevailing in indigenous areas, would also prove difficult to manage and to delimit in practice.

At the same time, the new constitution proclaimed a 'plural

economy' with different forms of ownership in the productive sphere: private, communitarian, cooperative and public. This reflected the diversity of forms of ownership in the country, but without much consideration for the contradictions between them. The uneasy relationship in the mines, for example, between public and private, and between unions (*sindicatos*) and 'cooperatives', was symptomatic of conflicting interests between different organized groups. It would prove difficult in practice for the state to manage the competing claims of different sorts of ownership, particularly at a time when high prices (e.g. for minerals) increased the intensity of competition between claimants. While the constitution reaffirmed the primacy of the state in the ordering and regulation of the economy (marking a sharp change from what had gone before), the lack of a precise legal framework made it easier for the private sector and cooperatives to take advantage of the situation to protect their interests.

The constitution also provided a new deal for indigenous peoples, setting guarantees for those living on Tierras Comunitarias de Orígen (TCOs or TIOCs) and the like. The land policies of the Morales government, building on and enhancing the INRA legislation it inherited, provided an important boost to land titling, favouring TCOs in particular. It is estimated that some 800,000 campesinos and indigenous people benefited from policies of *saneamiento*. But these policies failed to resolve the problems of unequal distribution of land. They left large estates in the east of the country intact while doing little to resolve the problem of landlessness (or very reduced landownership) that afflicted much of the campesino population, particularly in the Altiplano. This problem of the inequities in landownership was to surface with force behind the TIPNIS dispute in 2011/12, a dispute that reflected differences in traditions of landownership between campesinos and indigenous communities. The TIPNIS dispute was to have a negative impact on the standing of the MAS administration, both domestically and internationally.

Further, while affirming indigenous rights and the notion of '*vivir bien*' as a guiding principle for harmonious living and the protection of the natural environment, it was unclear how this was to mesh with the traditional role of extractive industries in the country and their importance in the economy. Bolivia remained highly dependent on extractive industries for the bulk of its tax revenues and export earnings. While the economic model pursued by the MAS administration after 2006 involved a significant shift away from that of laissez-faire and privatization introduced in the 1990s, it did not create an alternative to the export-led growth model reaffirmed at that time, except insofar as it sought to industrialize, where possible, the production of raw materials – basically gas and minerals. In fact, with rents from extractives used as the basis for redistribution, the incentives to keep within the model were arguably reinforced.

The conflict between extractive industry on the one hand and the protection of indigenous peoples and their natural environment on the other was perhaps clearest in the case of Tarija, the source of around 80 per cent of Bolivia's gas earnings. Although indigenous groupings had managed to gain compensation in some instances from foreign gas-producing companies, they had done so without any involvement by the state or public policy. The state found itself confronting a dilemma: needing to attract foreign investment and technology to develop its extractive industries and thus boost exports, while at the same time finding itself under pressure to protect the natural environment and the habitat of indigenous peoples. On balance, when push came to shove, the needs of the former seemed to prevail. Under the constitution, the state has a responsibility to ensure consultation with indigenous peoples before proceeding with extractive projects (both hydrocarbons and mining), and the government has yet to play a proactive role in this regard. Conditions within TCOs where extractive projects are taking place remain little changed, and indigenous peoples have yet to reap the benefits where such projects are taking place on their lands.

The need to guarantee food supplies to an increasingly urbanized population also created difficulties in public policy. With most of Bolivia's food now originating in Santa Cruz, much of it produced by agro-industrial concerns, government policy found itself being forced into negotiations with these powerful interests at the expense of its professed social goals. This certainly had a constraining influence on land policy in Santa Cruz. At the same time, the government failed to take steps to ease problems of land pressure on the Altiplano or to enhance the productive potential of small-scale producers in the highlands, one of its core sources of political support. With large numbers of peasant farmers unable to sustain themselves or their families on minute plots of increasingly degraded land, there was little alternative but for them to continue processes of migration to the cities or to seek land on the agricultural frontier in the Oriente. Thus the objective of tackling poverty where this was most acute – on the Altiplano – was not broached in such a structural way as to raise the productive and marketing capacities of peasant producers. Rather the option appeared to be to rely on agribusiness to meet the food needs of an increasingly urbanized society.

Similarly, creating a better distribution of income was one of the key promises of the Morales administration when it took office. Bolivia remained one of Latin America's most unequal countries in terms of income, and one of the government's objectives was to raise the proportion of income in the hands of the poor. It sought, in particular, to take control of strategic industries and to use these to channel resources towards deprived and vulnerable populations. Similarly, land policy was geared towards correcting distortions in ownership; there is little doubt that policies of *saneamiento* and land titling contributed to boosting living standards among some sectors of the rural poor. But, as we have seen, the scope for improved land distribution was limited. At the same time, the government resorted to subsidies designed to improve living standards of targeted groups (such as nursing mothers, schoolchildren and the elderly), funding these mainly from the proceeds of increased taxation on hydrocarbons and mineral production. But while there were transfers of wealth, such policies were contingent on the maintenance of tax revenues. There were also evident inequalities in the share-out of this greatly increased fiscal cake between departments. To tackle poverty, more thought would need to be given to developing specific policies to this end, e.g. policies to favour small-scale producers in rural areas like the Altiplano and unemployed people living in poor neighbourhoods of the cities.

Meanwhile, the public sector – the recipient of far greater re-sources than had ever been the case in the past – found itself unable to spend much of the money at its disposal. This was something of a novel situation for a country in which the public sector (or large parts of it) had been starved of cash for decades. The administrative capacity to handle these resources was sadly lacking at all levels of government. As we saw in the case of Tarija, administrative controls designed to reduce corruption had the effect of reducing spending even when the money was available. And finally, poor administration and the lack of effective public oversight meant that corruption continued to be a common problem.

The issue of decentralization posed yet another set of problems for the government. The demand for regional autonomies brought the country to the brink of civil conflict in 2008. The administration had initially sought to oppose autonomies, believing – probably correctly – that these were just a pretext by which local elites (especially in the Oriente) sought to wrest control of prerogatives vested in central government, particularly with respect to land reform. However, the constitution finally recognized the need for autonomies, introducing a complex system of decentralization to departments, municipalities and indigenous areas, and to specific regions like the Chaco. The competences achieved, however, were less far reaching than the '*media luna*' had fought for. By 2012, the extent of real decentralization was constrained by difficulties in setting up this new multi-tiered system. Different levels of administration experienced difficulties in establishing the relevant statutes or *cartas orgánicas*. Even municipalities that had opted to reconstitute themselves as 'indigenous' were having difficulties in this respect, balancing the interests of different social groups within them. The extent to which the central government was keen to pursue this agenda was always open to doubt; decentralizing powers and responsibilities at the expense of central government could well create rather than resolve problems of governability.

The question of autonomies, indeed, highlighted the more general problem of the relationship between the state and organized civil society. As we saw at the outset of this book, Bolivia has long had a relatively strong and well-organized civil society, though its ability to stand up for itself has varied according to different political contexts. At the same time, the authority and reach of the state have been weak overall, at least in comparison with other Latin American countries. The relationship between state and civil society has clearly undergone important changes in recent times, with the latter significantly empowered, at least during the first five years of the new millennium. Since the victory of Morales in 2005, social movements have gained access to the state in ways that were unprecedented, with the leaders of social movements taking up important functions of government. However, by the same token, we have noted here how, in several contexts, this seems to have led to a process of demobilization and atomization of social movements. We have analysed the reasons for this, stressing problems such as the absorption of social leaders into public administration and the absence of a common agenda (particularly after the approval of the new constitution). It may also be the case that social movements find it difficult to maintain themselves in a state of mobilization indefinitely, unless the circumstances demand it. If people feel that the government is 'theirs', then they feel less need to be constantly vigilant. The role of social organizations is principally to defend the interests of those that form them, although on occasions (as in the gas war) their agenda becomes much wider. In neither case, however, does this necessarily coincide with the functions of running a country. Within government, leaders recruited from social movements found themselves straddling a sometimes difficult divide, responsive both to pressures from above (the government) and from below (their grassroots membership). It proved difficult to rally people to advance their causes and at the same time to involve themselves in government with all the pressures that this implies. In practice, it seems that the notion of social control, both within the constitution and more broadly, has been put on the back burner.

At the same time, a lack of political coordination between such movements meant that there was a process of fragmentation between and within them: increasingly they came to fight for their own sectional interests rather than – as they had prior to 2006 – push for political change across the board. The breakdown of the Pacto de Unidad in 2010 and 2011 took this process further, driving a wedge between those rural social movements still aligned to the government (campesinos, *colonizadores* and Bartolinas) and those adopting a more independent stance (indigenous movements from both the highlands and lowlands). The latter, in any case, had always maintained a greater distance from government than the former. Rifts between social organizations, such as between unionized mineworkers and *cooperativistas*, or between *sindicatos* and *ayllus* on the Altiplano, seemed, in the long run, likely to further weaken social movements as a whole and reduce their capacity to act as 'motors' of change.

So the new constitution helped resolve a number of deeply rooted contradictions in Bolivian society, but it gave rise to new tensions and conflicts. This is hardly surprising. Seeking to implement the constitution, the second Morales administration was assailed by significant groups which felt that their interests had not been taken properly into account. Managing these conflicts – of which there were many in the six months in which the research for this book was conducted – was to prove taxing and debilitating for the government. The true significance of 'the processes of change' we have alluded to here is difficult to assess in the long sweep of history; it will take several decades for the dust to settle and for a definitive interpretation to emerge. However, it is our guess that the changes that took place in these years will be seen by future generations as key to the overall direction of events over the forthcoming years. Whatever happens, there will be no return to the status quo.

INTERVIEWEES

César Aguilar, Cobija, Pando
Lourdes Aguilar, Mujeres en Acción, Tarija
Xavier Albó, CIPCA, La Paz
Edgar Amutari, Cirabo, Riberalta, Beni
Francisco Añaguaya, Central Agraria, Huarina, La Paz
Juanita Ancieta, Seis Federaciones, Cochabamba
Darwin Araujo, Cobija, Pando
Helena Argirakis, Santa Cruz
Isabel Atencio, Urbanización 18 de Mayo, El Alto
Alejandra Avenante Montero, APG Caraparí, Tarija
Juan José Avila, Desafío, Santa Cruz
José Bailaba, Organización Indígena Chiquitana, Concepción, Santa Cruz
Justa Cabrera, *sub-alcalde*, Santa Cruz
Alfredo Cahuaya, IIADI, El Alto
Marco Calderón de la Barca, Empresa Minera San Cristóbal, La Paz
Cristina Callaú, COD, Riberalta, Beni
Enrique Camargo, Camiri, Santa Cruz
Carol Carlo, Universidad Amazónica, Cobija, Pando
Calixto Cartagena, Organización Indígena Caviñenos de la Amazonía, Riberalta, Beni
Luis Morgan Casey, bishop of Riberalta, Beni
Faustina Casillas, Federación del Trópico, Villa Tunari, Cochabamba
Satuco Castaño, Central Agraria, Huarina, La Paz
Jhonny Castillo Mamani, Iskaya, Ancoraimes, La Paz
Joaquín Castillo Mamani, Iskaya, Ancoraimes, La Paz
Mario Castillo, Villa Tunari, Cochabamba

Miguel Castro, Avina, Tarija
Adisol Chávez, Federación Bartolina Sisa, Cobija, Pando
José Chávez, Plan 3000, Santa Cruz
Lucy Chicunavi, Federación Fabriles, Riberalta, Beni
Elen Chillimani, Plan 3000, Santa Cruz
Raquel Chipana, COSLAM, Shinahota, Cochabamba
Teodoro Choque Chila, Jakisa, Challapata, Oruro
Eva Colque, Fundación Nuna, La Paz
Gonzalo Colque, Fundación Tierra, La Paz
José Luis Colque, Radio Kawsachun Coca, Lauca Ñ, Cochabamba
Mercedes Condori, formerly of Fejuve, Distrito 4, El Alto
Eduardo Correa, former sub-mayor, Plan 3000, Santa Cruz
Jorge Cortés, CEADESC, Cochabamba
Kendy Cortés, Federación Bartolina Sisa, Riberalta, Beni
Guido Cortéz, Cer-det, Tarija
Miguel Angel Crespo, Probioma, Santa Cruz
Andrea Cutili, Iskaya, Ancoraimes, La Paz
Alejandro Dausá, Desafío, Santa Cruz
Gladys Eamara, Federación Bartolina Sisa, Riberalta, Beni
Alberto Echazú, Comibol, La Paz
Susana Eróstegui, UNITAS, La Paz
Celia Espezo Lázaro, Jakisa, Challapata, Oruro
Juan de Díos Fernández, INRA, La Paz
Gualberto Flores, Foro Vecinal, Santa Cruz
Manuel Flores, councillor, Huarina, La Paz

Ruth Franco, Federación Bartolina Sisa, Riberalta, Beni

Justina Galván Calle, Jakisa, Challapata, Oruro

Erlan Gamarra, Empresa Boliviana de Almendra, Riberalta, Beni

Gerardo Garrett, Asociación de Mineros Privados, La Paz

Basilia Gerónimo Oxza, Jakisa, Challapata, Oruro

Javier Gómez, CEDLA, La Paz

Hermán Gonzáles, Federación de Periodistas, Riberalta, Beni

Edwin Grimaldo, St Andrew's College, Plan 3000, Santa Cruz

Sinforoso Gutiérrez, Janka Jahuira Chico, Huarina, La Paz

Pascal Huallpa, Jakisa, Challapata, Oruro

Rudy Huayllas, Jatun Killaka Asanajaqi, Challapata, Oruro

Mauro Hurtado, Cipca, Camiri, Santa Cruz

Raúl Kieffer, Cámara Boliviana de Hidrocarburos y Energía, Santa Cruz

Anastasio Lázaro, Jakisa, Challapata, Oruro

Roxana Liendo, formerly vice-minister of rural development, La Paz

Mónica Lijerón, CEJIS, Riberalta, Beni

Manuel Lima, former general secretary of Federación Campesina, Cobija, Pando

Pilar Lizárraga, Jaina Research Institute, Tarija

Marcos Llanos, IIADI, El Alto

Feliciano López Mamani, Iskaya, Ancoraimes, La Paz

Tomás Magme, Plan 3000, Santa Cruz

Armando Mamani, Cotacota Alta, Huarina, La Paz

Artemio Mamani, Federación Regional de Cooperativas Mineras del Norte de Potosí, Llallagua

Fernanda Mamani, Iskaya, Ancoraimes, La Paz

Oscar Mamani Paco, Collana, La Paz

Severino Mamani, Janka Jahuira Chico, Huarina, La Paz

Antonio Maraza, Jakisa, Challapata, Oruro

Sixto Marca Torrez, Jakisa, Challapata, Oruro

Noemí Marigua, Federación Bartolina Sisa, Riberalta, Beni

Elmer Matías, Organización Indígena Caviñenos de la Amazonía, Riberalta, Beni

Eduardo Mendoza, ACLO, Tarija

Virgilio Mendoza Marce, Jakisa, Challapata, Oruro

Carlos Hugo Molina, CEPAD, Santa Cruz

Damaris Monje, Federación Bartolina Sisa, Riberalta, Beni

César Navarro, vice-minister for social movements, La Paz

Jacqueline Negrete, Federación de Fabriles, Riberalta, Beni

Fanny Nina, former president of Fejuve, El Alto

Marcos Nordgren, CIPCA, Riberalta, Beni

Dionicio Núñez, vice-minister for coca and integral development, La Paz

Eulogio Núñez, CIPCA, Santa Cruz

Juan Carlos Núñez, Fundación Jubileo, La Paz

Basilio Oporto, Cooperativa Multiactiva, Llallagua

Segundina Orellano, Mariscal Sucre B, Villa Tunari, Cochabamba

Enrique Ormachea, CEDLA, La Paz

Víctor Pacosilla, managing director, CITY, El Alto

Mariel Paz, former *Defensora del Pueblo* (ombudsman), Tarija

Osvaldo Peñafiel, Desafío, Santa Cruz

José Pimentel, Comibol, La Paz

Rosa Quete, CAIC, Riberalta, Beni

Freddy Quilo, Parroquia Santa María de los Pobres, El Alto

Rolando Quiroga, Tarija

Tomás Quiroz, mayor of Llallagua, Potosí

Cleo Quispe, Achocalla, La Paz

Hipólito Quispe, student, UPEA, El Alto
Marcelino Quispe López, Jakisa,
    Challapata, Oruro
Benito Ramos Callisaya, deputy for
    Potosí
David Ramos, FSTMB, La Paz
Ana Lucia Reis, mayoress of Cobija,
    Pando
Carlos Revilla, UNITAS, La Paz
Juan Fernando Reyes, Herencia, Cobija,
    Pando
Guillermo Rioja, Ecomingas, Universidad
    Amazónica, Cobija, Pando
Antonia Rodríguez, Asarbolsem, Primero
    de Mayo, El Alto
Juan Carlos Rojas, formerly INRA,
    Cochabamba
Asterio Romero, departmental
    government, Cochabamba
Ciro Rosado, Tarija
Roberto Ruiz, departmental government,
    Tarija
Hugo Salvatierra, former agriculture
    minister, Santa Cruz
Godofredo Sandóval, PIEB, La Paz
Isaac Sandóval Rodríguez, Santa Cruz
Marcelo Sapiencia, Empresa Boliviana de
    Almendra, Riberalta, Beni
Moisés Sapirenda, Capitán General,
    Pueblo Weenhayek, Caparandita,
    Tarija
Verónica Segarrundo, former student,
    UPEA, El Alto
Andrés Segundo, APG, Entre Ríos, Tarija
Sarela Sejas, CIPCA, Cobija, Pando

Marfa Silva, Plan 3000, Santa Cruz
Limberth Siriora, Federación de Fabriles,
    Riberalta, Beni
Lorenzo Soliz, CIPCA Nacional, La Paz
Norma Soliz, Santiago II, El Alto
Carlos Soria, La Paz
Adriana Soto, CEADESC, Cochabamba
Gustavo Soto, CEADESC, Cochabamba
Alison Spedding, UMSA, La Paz
Arminda Súñiga, Huarina, La Paz
Leonardo Tamborini, CEJIS, Santa Cruz
Andrea Ticona, Iskaya, Ancoraimes, La
    Paz
Eufronio Toro, CIPCA, Camiri, Santa
    Cruz
María Luisa Urrelo, Parroquia Santa
    María de los Pobres, El Alto
Carlos Vacaflores, Jaina Research
    Institute, Tarija
Alcides Vadillo, Fundación Tierra, Santa
    Cruz
Olivio Vargas, Jakisa, Challapata, Oruro
Jorge Velázquez, Diakonía, La Paz
Dora Villanueva, Potosí
Juani Watayca, Federación Bartolina
    Sisa, Riberalta, Beni
Elizabeth Yucra, Federación Tupaj Katari,
    Villa Tunari, Cochabamba
Alfredo Yujra, Distrito 4, El Alto
Justino Zambrana, president of the
    departmental assembly, Tarija
Miguel Zubieta, formerly miners' union
    general secretary, Huanuni
Leonilda Zurita, Federación del Trópico,
    Cochabamba

FURTHER READING

English titles

Artaraz, Kepa (2011) *Bolivia: The Refounding of the Nation*, London: Pluto Press.

Chaplin, Ann (2010) 'Social movements in Bolivia: from strength to power', *Community Development Journal*, 45(3).

Crabtree, John (2005) *Patterns of Protest: Politics and Social Movements in Bolivia*, London: Latin America Bureau.

Crabtree, John and Laurence Whitehead (eds) (2008) *Unresolved Tensions: Bolivia Past and Present*, Pittsburgh, PA: University of Pittsburgh Press.

Harten, Sven (2011) *The Rise of Evo Morales and the MAS*, London: Zed Books.

Humphreys Bebbington, Denise (2010) 'Anatomy of a regional conflict: Tarija and resource grievances in Morales' Bolivia', *Latin American Perspectives*, 37(4).

Hylton, Forrest and Sinclair Thomson (2007) *Revolutionary Horizons: Past and Present in Bolivian Politics*, London: Verso.

John, Sandor (2009) *Bolivia's Radical Tradition: Permanent Revolution in the Andes*, Tucson: University of Arizona Press.

Klein, Herbert S. (2011) *A Concise History of Bolivia*, vol. 2, Cambridge: Cambridge University Press.

Kohl, Benjamin and Linda Farthing (2006) *Impasse in Bolivia: Neoliberal Hegemony and Popular Resistance*, London: Zed Books.

Lazar, Sian (2008) *El Alto, Rebel City*, Durham, NC: Duke University Press.

Pearce, Adrian (ed.) (2011) *Evo Morales and the Movimiento al Socialismo in Bolivia: The First Term in Context*, London: Institute for the Study of the Americas/Bolivia Information Forum.

Shultz, Jim and Melisa Crane Draper (eds) (2008) *Dignity and Defiance: Stories from Bolivia's Challenge to Globalization*, Pontypool: Merlin Press.

Sivak, Martín (2010) *Evo Morales: The Extraordinary Rise of the First Indigenous President of Bolivia*, Basingstoke: Palgrave.

Spanish titles

Albó, Xavier (2008) *Movimientos y poder indígena en Bolivia, Ecuador y Perú*, La Paz: CIPCA.

Arze, Carlos et al. (2011) *Gasolinazo: subvención popular al Estado y a las petroleras*, La Paz: CEDLA.

CEADESC (2008) *Atlas de Contratos petroleros en tierras comunitarios de origen y municipios de Bolivia*, Santa Cruz: CEADESC.

Chumacero, Juan Pablo et al. (2011) *Informe 2010: Territorios Indígena Originario Campesinos en Bolivia, entre la Loma Santa y la Pachamama*, La Paz: Fundación Tierra.

Eyzaguirre, José Luis (2005) *Composición de los ingresos familiares de campesinos indígenas. Un estudio en seis regiones de Bolivia*, La Paz: CIPCA.

Gray Molina, George (ed.) (2007) *El estado del Estado en Bolivia*, La Paz: PNUD.

Hinojosa, Leonith (ed.) (2012) *Gas y Desarrollo: Dinámicas territoriales rurales en Tarija – Bolivia*, La Paz: Fundación Tierra/Cer-det.

Liendo, Roxana (2009) *Participación Popular y el Movimiento Campesino Aymara*, La Paz: CIPCA/AIPE/ Fundación Tierra.

Mamani Pacasi, Rolando et al. (2012) *Vivir Bien. Significados y representaciones desde la vida cotidiana (cuatro miradas)*, La Paz: U-PIEB.

Revilla, Carlos (2007) *Visibilidad y Obrismo: La Estrategía del Plan Progreso en la Cuidad de El Alto*, La Paz: UNITAS.

Spedding, Alison and Abraham Colque (2003) *Nosotros los yungueños: testimonios de los yungueños del siglo XX*, La Paz: PIEB/Ediciones Mama Huaco.

Urioste, Miguel (2010) *Concentración y extranjerización de la tierra en Bolivia*, La Paz: Fundación Tierra.

Vacaflores, Carlos et al. (2005) *Conflicto y colaboración en el manejo de recursos naturales (experiencias de Bolivia y Argentina)*, La Paz: JAINA/ Plural.

Zuazo, Moira (2008) *Como nació el MAS? La ruralización de la política en Bolivia*, La Paz: Fundación Friedrich Ebert.

INDEX